LAWYERS'
LATIN

LAWYERS' LATIN

A VADE·MECUM

new edition

JOHN GRAY, BA Oxon
of the Inner Temple, Barrister, Quondam Recorder

ROBERT HALE · LONDON

ISBN 978 0 7090 8277 4

Robert Hale Limited
Clerkenwell House
Clerkenwell Green
London EC1R 0HT

www.halebooks.com

A catalogue record for this book is available from the British Library

6   8   10   9   7   5

Typeset by Derek Doyle and Associates, Shaw Heath
Printed and bound by the MPG Books Group, Bodmin and King's Lynn

Contents

To my wife Susan
Auditque vocatus Apollo

Et cani ingenti Bertie equoque uxoris meae Apollo –
'and to my very big dog, Bertie, and to
my wife's horse, Apollo'

Acknowledgements

My thanks go to those identified below for permission to use material more particularly detailed in the text as follows:

Sweet and Maxwell Ltd for passages from *Trial by Jury* by Sir Patrick Devlin, material from the 1973 Reports of Patent Cases, from 9, *Law Quarterly Review*, from Glanville Williams's *Learning the Law*, 11th edition, 1982, p. 60, from Archbold, *Pleading, Evidence and Practice in Criminal Cases*, 38th edition, 1973, and from the Civil Procedure Rules 2005.

Lexis Nexis Butterworths Tolley for passages from Radcliffe and Cross, *The English Legal System*, 3rd edition, 1954, by G.R.Y. Radcliffe D.C.L. and Geoffrey Cross MA, from Cheshire and Fifoot, *Law of Contract*, 4th edition, 1965, by G.C. Cheshire and C.H.S. Fifoot, and *Cross on Evidence*, 1958 edition, p. 30, by Rupert Cross MA.

The Penguin Group (UK) for a passage from *Six Great Advocates* by Lord Birkett, Penguin Books, 1961.

Sir Gavin Lightman for an extract from his Chancery Bar Association spring lecture 1998 published as an article in *The Times* on 9th June 1998 entitled 'Bumping Over the Silk Road'.

The Times (© Times Newspapers Limited) for an extract from the leader column of 9th January 2001, information reported by *The Sunday Times*, April 2000, column headings from *The Times*, 29th January 1999, 19th July 2000 and a law report (*Fryer* v *Pearson*) 4th April 2000.

Parliamentary copyright material from Hansard, and Statutes reproduced with permission of the Controller of Her Majesty's Stationary Office on behalf of Parliament.

The *Daily Telegraph* for an extract from an article of 20th April 1999, 'Plain English at the Heart of Legal Reform' by Terence Shaw.

Sir Christopher Staughton for an extract from the Fifth Millennium Lecture 'What's Wrong With The Law 2000' delivered 29th November 2000 to the Inner Temple; and for two Latin maxims which emanated from his court.

The Provost and Scholars of King's College, Cambridge, and the Society of Authors as the literary representatives of the estate of E. M. Forster for a sixteen-word extract from *Abinger Harvest*.

I record a generalized thanks for the back-up assistance derived from regular consultation of the following:

Kennedy's *Revised Latin Primer*, Longman Group Limited, 1962.
New Pocket Dictionary of Latin and English Languages compiled by J. Macfarlane published undated (but pre-1958) by Eyre and Spottiswood Publishers Ltd, London.
A Dictionary of Latin Words and Phrases by James Morwood (Oxford University Press, 1998).
A Dictionary of Law, 4th edition, edited by Elizabeth A. Martin (Oxford University Press, 1997).
Osborne's Concise Law Dictionary, 8th edition, edited by Leslie Rutherford and Sheila Bone (Sweet and Maxwell Ltd, 1993).
The Oxford Compact English Dictionary edited by Catherine Soanes (Oxford University Press, 2003)
The Oxford Modern English Dictionary edited by Julia Swannell (Oxford University Press, 1992).
Chambers Twentieth Century Dictionary, 1974 edition, edited by A.M. Macdonald OBE (BA Oxon, 1974).
The Supreme Court Practice 1988 (Sweet and Maxwell and Stevens and Sons).
A Dictionary of Latin Tags and Phrases by Eugene Ehrlich (Robert Hale, 1989): a volume which I have owned for a long time and which was influential in determining how I would write *Lawyers' Latin*.

I extend my heartfelt thanks to all those concerned with the granting of copyright permissions. Without exception, they were patient, helpful and accommodating.

Finally, thanks to my wife, Susan, for drawing my very big dog, Bertie, and her horse, Apollo.

Foreword

When I began my working life on the true blue *Morning Post* in 1931, members of the editorial staff were encouraged to throw in a Latin tag where appropriate. Later in the century, while I was editing the *Daily Telegraph* 1975–1986, the leader writers were still free to use a Latin phrase if it helped them to express what they wanted to convey.

A leading article, for example, about misconduct in a police force sat up and begged for the heading: *Quis custodiet ipsos custodes*? How better to express it? The duller English equivalent is, 'Who guards the guards?' A leading article on our loss of school playing fields? *Mens sana in corpore sano* cuts a lot more ice than 'a healthy mind in a healthy body', which sounds faintly patronising. Greek texts, on the other hand, were always strongly discouraged – simply because the printers charged so much more for setting Greek.

If readers wrote, as they sometimes did, complaining of some howler in the newspaper, I found that a hand-written card – *Mea culpa, maxima culpa . . .*! usually provided satisfaction. There are many areas where Latin can express the point you want to make more pungently than any other language. Try to translate *quo vadis*? into German – or even English – and you will see the advantages of occasional resort to Latin.

Horace has always seemed to me among the most expressive of the Latin poets. *Nil desperandum Teucro duce et auspice Teucro.* We can drop the Teucro bit, but *Nil desperandum* has a ring about it (even in a rugby scrum when the score against you is 5–25) which no other language can match.

Dulce et decorum est pro patria mori, Horace sang; or rather less elegantly: 'It is a sweet and honourable thing to die for your country.' Such sentiments are unfashionable these days; but a lot of the generation which failed to return from the First World War understood Horace's message.'

Now and again, meeting a long lost friend, I exclaim *Eheu fugaces, Postume, Postume. Labuntur anni*, otherwise, 'Ah me, Postumus, Postumus, the fleeting years are slipping by . . .' How well that conveys the passing years and all that slips so quickly away as we grow older. How better to greet an old friend whom you have not seen for a long time? That's Horace again.

You might suppose, if you have read so far, that all this is a bit of showing off by someone lucky enough to have had an expensive education which incorporated the classics. Not a bit of it! I left my public school in 1929, a year early, with relatively little learning, after my father had caught a severe chill in the Wall Street crash of that year. But I had taken in just sufficient Latin to perceive its uses.

And as I proceeded through life and made a living out of writing for a newspaper, I saw increasingly that the little Latin I had gleaned enabled me occasionally to express myself as no other language could. Alas, no more. That mode of expression is out. Latin tags in leading articles, no matter how expressive, would today be condemned as elitist, would lead to angry letters from the readers and would probably lose the newspaper circulation.

That is a loss for several reasons. A little knowledge of Latin, it seems to me, is also a useful reminder that although the ancients were without so much that we have today – the jet aircraft, the modern Tate, the mobile telephone, Internet, precision bombing and Channel 4 – they possessed a certain wisdom and a gift for conveying it which is beyond us today. So I find what little Latin I know and understand rather humbling. It brings home to me that I am not half as clever or as wise as I would like to think I am. Somebody thought what I think now a couple of thousand or more years ago and expressed it with greater clarity than I can muster – though I earn my living as a wordsmith.

Sadly, however, there has developed a view among people who think correctly and govern our lives that far from inculcating humility even a frail grasp and occasional use of Latin conveys superiority. So a well-worn Latin phrase such as *pro bono publico* – a cliché, if ever there was one – smacks of toffdom and must be placed out of bounds.

I am not qualified to say whether Latin remains an indispensable tool of trade for the legal profession. Nor can I tell you – as an Anglican – how far the virtual abandonment of the Roman Catholic Mass in Latin reduces the chances of eternal life. But as a journalist I know that putting Latin beyond the pale has reduced my options; it has narrowed my way of conveying what I wish to say.

In a letter to a newspaper recently a reader wrote in defence of the Turner Prize that it represented a level of art that ordinary people without much talent could achieve. Great artists of the past – all of them beyond most people's reach, so not for these times. That helps us to understand why Latin is out of favour.

Let me finally illustrate the value of another tongue with an expression carved, not from the Latin but from the French. *Tout casse, tout passe, tout lasse*. Everything breaks, everything passes, everything dies. There's our life. How better to express it? Even Horace could not have conveyed the human tragedy so well.

Rt. Hon. The Lord Deedes of Aldington KBE, MC, PC, DL

Preface

'Legal Latin outlawed *pro bono publico*'. This news headed a column in *The Times* for 29th January, 1999. Proposed was the abolition of familiar legal Latin by the Civil Procedure Rules (CPR) from 26th April, 1999, when these superseded the Rules of The Supreme Court (RSC).

Official onslaught against use of Latin in the law quickly gathered momentum. 'People should stop using maxims or doctrines dressed up in Latin, such as *res ipsa loquitur*, which are not readily comprehensible to those for whose benefit they are supposed to exist', said Lord Justice May (*Fryer* v *Pearson, The Times*, 4th April, 2000. 'Judicial disapproval of Latin Maxims'). Then came: 'Throw Latin out of Court' (*The Times*, 19th July 2000) echoing Lord Woolf. He told the American Bar Association that already he had promoted the scrapping of Latin in the civil courts to help public understanding of the process. 'I hope that the same will apply in the criminal courts,' he added, before announcing that he would abolish *certiorari* (see text): it would be called a 'quashing order'.

Latin usage is to be forbidden in the courts, ostensibly to make the law more comprehensible and less intimidating to lay people, *ad captandum vulgus* (see text). Yet botanists, and those concerned in industry with fragrances derived from plants, revere it as an international language by which species are named and can be identified. Nobody there suggests change because the practice might be thought elitist and offend the average gardener's sensitivities. Entomologists (insects) and ichthyologists (fish) too are happy to classify in Latin.

For reasons set out below, the elimination of Latin would not for some considerable time obviate difficulty for those young lawyers who have little or no knowledge of the language. At the same time the process will inconvenience (and frequently annoy) their seniors, who must adapt to, live and work with changes to what they find second nature. It will be intolerable and time-wasting for them to be interrupted and admonished whenever Latin slips out.

Latin was the language of official documents, and maxims were derived from Roman law or invented by medieval jurists, so that many expressions are now deeply woven into the fabric of the law. Translation can be unsatisfactory and lengthy. Often, too, the Latin is no more than a label identifying a principle or body of law which must be researched, even by the professional. To change the label serves no practical purpose, particularly when the name on the label is known already to so many and the new label means little or nothing to the layman and sometimes, initially, to the lawyer. In a few cases satisfactory translation (literal or at all) is virtually impossible, e.g., *de bene esse* (see text).

What value Lord Woolf's change from *certiorari* to 'quashing order'? *Certiorari* was quite as good a label for what was referred to. To the man in the street the one expression is as meaningless as the other. Latin apart, if public understanding of the legal process is one main objective of the massive changes currently being wrought in the law, some of those made by the CPR are astounding. The expressions 'Third Party Proceedings' and 'Payment into Court' clearly indicate the nature of their subject matter: yet they must give way respectively to 'Part 20 Claim' and 'Part 36 Payment'!

Frequently Latin is a useful and pithy shorthand: a tool of the legal profession. Qualification in a discipline involves learning to use the tools of the trade. If one, never apprenticed, cannot use the tools, ought they to be changed for the sake of change and public relations, often to be replaced by less good or less efficient tools? Changed so that those who do not need to use them may sometimes acquire a greater but generally imprecise, unnecessary and largely valueless understanding?

Not many now learn Latin in school, and Roman law (with original text or at all) is not compulsory in most universities for those reading law. Young lawyers may think that they welcome Latin's demise, but they will not now readily learn legal Latin in the course of their work. Yet they will continue to meet it in pre-2000 reported cases (but not necessarily so. Lord Hoffmann's speech in *Arthur J.S. Hall and co.* v *Simons* [2000] 3 WLR 543 p. 557 et seq., a landmark case, essential reading for all students, is not wanting for Latin content), in text books, in academic articles and in some old statutes (is *Magna Carta* to be translated and its real name abandoned?). Some of the younger members of the profession will find themselves ill-equipped. With them in mind, I compiled a list of Latin expressions prevalent in the law as it was circa 1999 with translation and, I hope, variously useful comment, guidance, interesting (sometimes entertaining) related information and example of usage. In order to produce a comprehensive handbook I have added to these a number of general Latin expressions and words likely to be encountered in the law, together with some which do not of themselves have immediate relevance to the law but which import accompanying information which is informative or of peculiar interest to lawyers. To attempt suppression of Latin in a civilized country is, in the scale of cultural atrocities, on a par with burning books.

Remember that Milton, Pope and Dryden, great masters of the English tongue, drew inspiration from Latin and translated Latin verse into English verse: and that Samuel Johnson (a resident of the Inner Temple, where today Dr Johnson's Buildings are named after him) declared that nothing would induce him to disgrace the walls of Westminster Abbey with an inscription in English.

I fear that I harbour the half-hope that among some this *vade-mecum* may stimulate not only an interest in but, conceivably, an affection for the Latin language. I should be delighted if its use were to realize the words of Cicero (found by chance in Kennedy's *Revised Latin Primer*): *haec studia adulescentiam alunt, senectutem oblectant* – these studies nurture youth and delight old age.

Might yet the wheel not turn full circle? Generations of budding lawyers will have learned from a footnote in Professor Glanville Williams's introductory book *Learning the Law* that in 1730 an Act was passed abolishing Law Latin in legal proceedings but that too many expressions were found, as Blackstone observed, to be 'not capable of an English dress with any degree of seriousness'. So, after two years, another Act was passed permitting the continued use of expressions 'in the same language as hath been commonly used'.

Legal decisions of the European Community's tribunals show no sign of shunning Latin. Two randomly selected reports between March 2000 and April 2001 contain the following: *ex officio, per se, ratione loci, lex fori, a fortiori* and *de facto*.*

The tolerant British should take care not to be neurotic, as the French are with 'Franglais'. The vilification of Latin is not matched by attack upon legal terminology derived from medieval French (from a time when Anglo-Norman was the language of the courts). What about *feoffment, laches, lien, autrefois convict/acquit, misfeasance, mesne, seisin, profit-à-prendre, venue, cestui que trust, chose in action, cy-près, in pais, executor de son tort, tenant pur autre vie, mortmain, puisne, replevin, voir dire,* etc.? Why discriminate against Latin?

Some judges are still happy to accept the use of familiar Latin terminology. Others think that use of Classical Greek should be introduced by way of rearguard action! When the Civil Procedure Rules came into force, the *Daily Telegraph* reported: 'Lord Woolf sweeps away the Latin phrases' and alerted the profession to some '2000 volunteers, who would monitor the courts to ensure that judges and lawyers stick to the new rules banning the old jargon'. Could this really be right? A culture of spying, sneaking and hot lines?

In *Dimond* v *Lovell* [2000] 2 WLR 1121 p. 1131–2, Lord Hoffmann found the expression *res inter alios acta* indispensable and used it three times, securing political correctitude once by the preface 'as one used to say'.

Deliberately listed are some English words and expressions, which, by the Civil Procedure Rules, have superseded Latin. The Latin follows each one, so that, if and when needed for research or other purposes, the old terminology may readily be traced. Also deliberately listed are a few medical expressions which many legal practitioners are likely to meet in medical reports and notes.

I have not dealt with pronunciation of Latin. For this I refer to and recommend James Morwood's *A Dictionary of Latin Words and Phrases* (Oxford University Press 1998).

* (1) *The Polo/Lauren Company, LP* v *PT Dwidua Langgeng,* etc., 6th April 2000. Court of Justice of European Communities (First Chamber) 2000 ETMR Issue 6. (2) Opinion of Advocate General Stix-Hackle delivered 5th April 2001 in *Zino Davidoff SA* v *inter alia Levi Strauss (UK) Ltd* v *inter alia Tesco PLC.*

My qualifications scarcely make me a Latin scholar. I have looked therefore to others better qualified and record my great debt and gratitude to the late Barry Nicholas, former Principal of Brasenose College, sometime Professor of Comparative Law and All Souls Reader in Roman Law in the University of Oxford; Sir Godfray Le Quesne QC; His Honour Judge John Weeks QC; Richard Gray QC; Nigel Hamilton QC; Angus Johnston, MA, LLM, BCL, tutor of Trinity Hall, Cambridge; Andrew Pugh QC; Elizabeth Skelton BCL, LLB (McGill); Barry Lewis MA, LLM, Solicitor; and Fiona Clark MA, for their time, effort, patience, input and invaluable advice, not by any means restricted to Latin translation. Final decision was however in all cases mine, as is all responsibility. My thanks also to my wife Susan, Jill Lloyd and Joc Phillips for interest, encouragement and proof reading. Thanks are further due to: Michael Oliver and James Donovan, senior clerks in my old chambers at 1 Crown Office Row, Temple, EC4, who have so generously and willingly continued to help me out in all sorts of ways related to the production of this book; to Mr John Hale of my publishers, Robert Hale Ltd, who has been endlessly patient with argument as to exactly which entries are appropriate and with an incessant stream of new material at the ever extended last minute and, last but not least, to those in the Inner Temple and Canterbury Cathedral libraries for ever willing assistance.

Finally: the dedication *Auditque vocatus Apollo* (Virgil Georgics iv. 7) 'and Apollo hears when called upon' needs explanation. Apollo is my wife's cherished horse.

John Gray
April 2002

Preface to New Edition

Since publication of *Lawyers' Latin* 31st July 2002 changes in the law and its administration have made some revision desirable and some essential (e.g., the abolition of the Lord Chancellor's Department). Before saying more I record my debt and thanks to Martin Bowley QC for his help in keeping me right on a number of matters in areas with which I had lost accurate and detailed touch, and to Howard Stevens for alerting me to relevant new cases.

There are also a few words and expressions, which have not been, but which perhaps ought to be included. Selection is not easy. There are a great many of what may be termed 'working' Latin tags, mottos, maxims and words, which might be incorporated (see e.g., Herbert Broom, *A Selection of Legal Maxims*, 10th edition, Sweet and Maxwell, 1939). I have, however, never sought to make this *vade-mecum* an exhaustive work. My objective has been to choose and insert in a short volume only those which have some real prospect of being encountered by legal practitioners or others who are in some way involved with the law, to whom the book is primarily directed. As appears below, just a few have been added with a view to providing light relief or amusement.

I have added an index of words and matters which appear in the text but may not be traceable where the Latin entry under which they appear is not remembered. This is by no means comprehensive and is intended as no more than a very general guide. Some additional cross-referencing too seemed advantageous.

Lawyers' Latin already contains material which reflects largely historical, literary or other incidental interest. Generally this is of little practical working use to the lawyer *qua* lawyer. However such material always touches upon the law, since at all times the criterion for inclusion has been whether it has a sufficient connection with the law to qualify as 'law-related Latin'. This includes diverting content intended to lighten the user's day. From those who have already acquired and utilized *Lawyers' Latin*, I have learned that this has been appreciated quite as much as the basic reference content. In reviewing for

The Times Literary Supplement on 14th February 2003, Justin Warshaw expressed the opinion that '*Lawyers' Latin* was a useful guide and entertaining enough to be read cover to cover'. I have therefore not hesitated to include more of the light-hearted. W.S. Gilbert (a barrister and member of the Inner Temple) is now a substantial contributor.

It is worth noting here that, after a long absence, Roman Law has been re-introduced as part of the syllabus for those reading jurisprudence at Oxford University, though not in as linguistically demanding a way as some may remember in the past. At the preliminary examination (Moderations) a compulsory 'Roman Introduction to Private Law' paper will not require any Latin; text from Gaius and Justinian having been studied in translation. For finals an optional paper in 'Roman Law (Delict)' will require comment on selected Latin texts but translation of them will not be asked.

I should too draw attention to the recent case of *Harding* v *Wealands* [2006] UKHL 32 in which the opinions of two of the law Lords were studded with a sufficient number of Latin expressions as to justify talk of revival.

A surprisingly large number of people, not in any way involved with its working usage, have an interest in the Latin of their law (in particular many will quote, with pleased amusement at their esoteric knowledge, *res ipsa loquitur* and *volenti non fit injuria*). They see it as a part of their heritage, eccentric perhaps but enjoyable.

I hope that *Lawyers' Latin* may be picked up and enjoyed by lawyer and layman alike. Our law belongs to us all. *Legum idcirco servi sumus ut liberi esse possumus* 'we are the bondsmen of the law so that we may be free'. Marcus Tullius Cicero 106–43 BC (an accolade for the rule of law). The current far-reaching and frightening threats to our freedoms, brought about by (over?) reaction to world terrorism, make it worthwhile perhaps to read and to ponder upon the commentary which follows the entries for *habeas corpus, judicium parium, Magna Carta, nulla poena sine lege, nulli vendemus, nullus liber homo* and *satius est impunitum*.

Lege feliciter 'read happily'.

John Gray
October 2006

How to Use this Vade-Mecum

The Latin entries appear alphabetically. They cater for the lawyer's working needs and are as short as possible, providing literal translation and sufficient to put the inquirer on track. In some cases there is further information and example, and sometimes a little more to lighten his day.

Non-lawyers may find it interesting and perhaps worthwhile to read what is too often regarded as exclusively for lawyers.

Note that a very few entries in English enable a Latin expression to be traced.

CPR refers to the Civil Procedure Rules, 1999.

In the text below the words 'he', 'him' and 'his' should be taken to include 'she' and 'her'.

Any Latin word beginning with a consonantal 'I' should be looked for under 'J'. There was no 'J' in the Latin language.

N.B. The English index is not exhaustive. It provides only for some of the words, names or matters which may be remembered from the text where the Latin entry under which they appear is not.

A

A bove majori discit arare minor 'a young ox learns to plough from an older one'. Applicable to apprenticeship or a barrister's pupillage.

See *fas est ab hoste doceri*.

Ab alio specta, alteri quod feceris 'look for the treatment you have meted out to others'. A warning that even the judiciary will one day face the Almighty.

See *nolite judicare*.

Ab honesto virum bonum nihil deterret 'nothing deters a good man from honesty (honour)'. Seneca. Is the old adage, that every man has his price, incorrect?

Ab initio 'from the start', from inception, from the beginning or the outset. The expression has a specific meaning in the law relating to trespass. Where a person, having entered upon land under a lawful authority, subsequently abuses that authority, his misbehaviour will relate back so as to make his original entry wrongful; so as to make him a trespasser *ab initio*. 'Where a man misdemeans himself or makes an ill use of the authority with which the law entrusts him, he shall be accounted a trespasser *ab initio*', Blackstone, *Comm.*, iii, p. 213. By the subsequent behaviour the law adjudges the intention with which a person initially entered the land. *The Six Carpenters' Case* [1610] Rep 146a, 146b.

Lord Denning invoked the doctrine in a matter involving mini-cab drivers touting for business at London Airport. 'These car-hire drivers abused the authority given to them by the law by hanging about and "touting", so they became trespassers from the beginning (*ab initio*) and can be turned out.' *Cinnamond* v *British Airport Authority* [1980] 2 All ER 368, 373. A trespass so brought about is termed a 'trespass *ab initio*'.

Absens haeres non erit 'the one who is absent will not be the heir (will not inherit)'. Out of sight out of mind.

Accedas in curiam 'you may come into court' . . . if in the year 2006 you can afford it. The cost of commencing proceedings in the High Court has recently escalated and legal aid continues to be further and further restricted. On 29 September 2005, *The Times* reported proposed huge increases in court fees. Furthermore lawyers just cannot accept 'no win no fee' cases where the financial outlay is too great and the prospects are uncertain (as they invariably are before the matter has been properly investigated and substantial money spent). There are few open and shut cases. Some see the entitlement to have litigation funded in this way as a cherry-pickers' charter.

'In England justice is open to all . . . like the Ritz Hotel', Lord Justice Sir James Mathew (1830–1908).

See *justitia omnibus* and *nulli vendemus*.

Acerrima proximorum odia 'the hatred of nearest relations is the most bitter'. Too often the experience of lawyers sorting out wills: evidently nothing new.

Accusare nemo se debet 'nobody is bound to incriminate himself'. In England a progressively eroded principle. Under The Judges' Rules 1964, once a police officer had reasonable grounds for suspecting that a person had committed an offence, he was bound to caution him before asking any or any further questions. Failure to do so jeopardized the prospective admissibility in evidence of any answers given.

The form of the required caution was: 'You are not obliged to say anything unless you wish to do so but what you say may be put into writing and given in evidence.' This has been changed to: 'You do not have to say anything but it may harm your defence if you do not mention when questioned something which you later rely on in court.' The right to silence at this early stage is now qualified.

The Exchange Control Act 1947 contained provision for the answering of questions under penalty and it appeared that the questions could be endlessly repeated and a fresh offence committed with each failure to answer. Some statutory powers (e.g., of the Department of Trade and Industry and of the Director of the Serious Fraud Office) which require answer to questions under penalty for refusal are draconian. As to the latter, see Criminal Justice Act 1987 and *Regina* v *Director of Serious Fraud Office ex parte Smith* [1992] 1 All ER 730 and 95 Cr App R 191.

It remains to be seen how far these powers may be affected by the provisions of the Human Rights Act 1998.

See *justitia omnibus, qui non negat confitetur* and *qui tacet consentit*.

Actio personalis moritur cum persona 'a person's right of action dies with the person'. Prior to the Law Reform (Miscellaneous Provisions) Act 1934 (and subject, since the first Fatal Accidents Act of 1846, to *sui generis* [see below] claims made under that Act broadly by dependants not themselves physically injured) it was cheaper to kill than to maim. This maxim survives, however, in the case of defamation.

Actus Dei nemini facit injuriam 'an act of God does a wrong to nobody'. Acts of God (e.g., earthquakes) do not in law constitute a wrong which gives a right to claim against anybody for consequential damage or injury suffered.

Actus reus Part of the maxim *actus non facit reum nisi mens sit rea*, 'an act does not make a person guilty unless his mind is guilty', which is a cardinal principle of English criminal law. Mental awareness or intent amounting to guilty mind is a necessary ingredient in making out nearly all crimes. *Actus reus* means a state of affairs prohibited by the criminal law and caused by the accused's act. The accused will, however, not be guilty unless there is also fault (*mens rea*, criminal mind or intent) on his part: generally speaking that is, some offences are absolute.

Ad captandum vulgus 'to win over the crowd'. Promises in the nature of bribery made by politicians, particularly in manifestos at election time, might be thought too often to be made *ad captandum vulgus*. A concept understood by the Countess of

Wessex and expressed in the disgracefully 'set up' tapes of April 2001. *The Sunday Times* reported her description of the Chancellor of the Exchequer's (Gordon Brown's) March budget as 'A nothing budget. . . . All for the election . . . a load of pap' (pap being soft food for children): applicable to abolition of Latin in the law?

Ad hoc 'to *or* for this'. For this specific purpose. A committee might be set up temporarily '*ad hoc*' to consider some matter . . . an *ad hoc* committee. Or there may be an *ad hoc* appointment.

Ad hominem 'to the person'. Relating to or associated with a particular person. In decision-making or argument, relying upon a person's emotions, characteristics or prejudices e.g., 'I don't accept his defence of greedy bankers: he's a greedy banker himself.' His views are *ad hominem*.

Ad horam 'to the hour', punctually.

Ad idem 'to the same', at one, coincidence of understanding. So in the fourth edition of Cheshire and Fifoot, *Law of Contract* at p. 46: 'in *Tinn* v *Hoffman and Co.* (in the Court of Exchequer Chamber) it was held by five judges against two that on the facts of that case no contract had been concluded. Of those in the majority Archibald and Keating JJ proceeded on the ground that the letters in question contained diverse terms so that the parties were not *ad idem*.'

Ad infinitum 'to infinity', without limit.

> So naturalists observe, a flea
> Hath smaller fleas that on him prey;
> And these have smaller fleas to bite 'em
> And so proceed *ad infinitum*.
>
> Jonathan Swift 1667–1745

Ad lib. Abbreviated version of *ad libitum*, meaning 'to plea-sure'. In English the expression *ad lib*. has come to refer to a speech or performance without planning or preparation: something improvised or spoken '*ex tempore*' (see below). It is also used in some restaurants, e.g., 'coffee *ad lib.*' meaning as many cups as desired with payment only for the first.

Ad litem 'for the suit *or* action'. Used in litigation e.g., 'guardian *ad litem*', a party appointed in a specific piece of litigation to supervise and look after the interests of a defendant who is under age or not of sound mind. The expression 'next friend' in the case of a plaintiff (claimant) was also used but both 'guardian *ad litem*' and 'next friend' are superseded by 'litigation friend' since the CPR replaced the Rules of the Supreme Court on 26th April, 1999.

Ad nauseam 'to nausea'. For example, His Lordship's judgement went on and on *ad nauseam*.

Ad referendum 'for further consideration'.

Ad rem 'to the matter *or* thing' in hand. Pertinent, to the point. *Nihil ad rem*, 'nothing to the matter in hand'; not to the point; irrelevant.

Ad unum omnes 'all to one'. All, to a man.

Ad valorem 'to value', in relation to or in proportion to value. An *ad valorem* duty or tax will vary according to the value of the item or matter taxed.

Adverso flumine 'against the stream'. Roman equivalent of uphill. The struggle is *adverso flumine* or uphill. Judge's interruptions make counsel's task *adverso flumine*. The opposite is *secundo flumine*, 'with the stream'.

Advocato suasus lingua Latina testificabor 'I am advised by counsel to give my evidence in Latin'. It might be unwise for counsel to give such advice. See *heu, modo*.

Advocatus 'advocate *or* lawyer'. In 1961, following a BBC series by Lord Birkett, Penguin Books published '*Six Great Advocates*'.

As Norman Birkett KC, the writer had himself been one of the great advocates of the twentieth century.

> I should like to conclude these sketches [of Sir Patrick Hastings KC, Sir Rufus Isaacs KC, Thomas Erskine and others] by saying something about the place of the advocate in our society . . . the advocate must be a student of words; he must know something of their history, their sound, their associations, and above all the use that has been made of them by great masters of the tongue. It is well if he knows the Bible in the authorized version (King James) and if he has made the language of the Book of Common Prayer his very own. It is well, too, if he knows something of the great triumvirate Chaucer, Shakespeare and Dryden who did so much to mould and fashion the language we speak, and of writers like Swift, Sterne and Defoe and other great stylists. For I am one of those who believe that in the ordinary everyday affairs of life, even in casual conversation, the use of graceful and simple English is an accomplishment greatly to be desired.

Yet in the schools not only is little or no Latin learned but rumour has it that literature at GCSE is to be downgraded in importance: and how often in the Established Church of England in 2006 is the language of the authorized King James Bible and the Book of Common Prayer to be heard? Will there be any more great orators and advocates?

See *Sanctus Ivo*.

Advocatus diaboli 'devil's advocate'. The name given by the Roman Catholic Church to an official formerly appointed to put the case against a proposed beatification or canonization. His opposite number was called *promotor fidei*, promotor of the faith. Contemporaneously with the last revision of the Code of Canon Law in 1983, Pope John Paul II abolished these offices and substituted an elaborate investigative procedure in which those questioned must include some who oppose the proposal. The canonists seem to have advised against the existing adversarial proceedure, familiar in English Law.

The expression 'devil's advocate' in popular usage has come to mean one who urges an opposite view; sometimes one who argues for the sake of argument, taking up an unpopular, absurd or unarguable standpoint.

Aequitas sequitur legem 'equity follows the law'. The Court of Chancery never maintained a right to ignore the Common Law as administered in the Courts of Common Pleas, Exchequer and King's/Queen's Bench. Equity followed the law and interfered only where the Common Law appeared to ignore some important factor or circumstance which bore upon the fairness of the matter before it.

Equity evolved a number of other labelling maxims including 'he who comes into equity must come with clean hands'. Though not seen in Latin, this merits mention. One who seeks to invoke equitable relief must show that he has not himself behaved badly in the transaction under scrutiny.

So in *Everet* v *Williams* [1725], noted in 9 LQR at p. 197, one highwayman found himself in difficulties with a partnership action for an account against another. The recitals in the bill recorded an oral partnership between the defendant and the plaintiff, who was 'skilled in dealing in several sorts of commodities', and that the parties, 'had proceeded jointly in the said dealings with good success on Hounslow Heath, where they dealt with a gentleman for a gold watch' and that the defendant had informed the plaintiff that 'Finchley was a good and convenient place to deal in and that the said commodities were very plenty at Finchley aforesaid'. Realizing the nature of the business, the court declared the claim 'scandal and impertinence'. The solicitors, William White and William Wreathcock, were summoned for contempt and taken into custody before being fined £50 each and consigned to the Fleet (the debtors' prison) until payment. The indignity to which the court had been subjected was declared to have been 'satisfyed by these fynes'. The felons, John Everet and Joseph Williams, were in due course hanged, respectively at Tyburn in 1730 and at Maidstone in 1727.

The description 'clean hands' has acquired a telling update: 'The dirty dog shall have no dinner here' (attributed to Sir

Charles Ritchie Russell).

See *qui prior est tempore potior est jure*, and *summa jus saepe summa injuria*.

Aequo animo 'with an equal mind'. With equanimity. The right judicial disposition. Composed: another desirable judicial quality.

See *boni viri*.

Affidavit 'he has sworn *or* stated on oath'. A written statement for use in court confirmed on oath. The opening words are: I (name) of (address), (occupation), make oath and say as follows: . . .' This word has survived the CPR and may still be used in limited circumstances.

See *jurat*.

A fortiori 'with stronger (reason or force)'. An *a fortiori* case is one, real or supposed, backed by an even stronger case (in reason or principle) than that under consideration. e.g., judges should not interrupt; *a fortiori* if they do not yet know anything about the case or: a man should be soundly punished for theft; *a fortiori* if he used violence.

Alea judiciorum 'the hazard of lawsuits'. Litigation hazard: something very real and to be considered seriously by all would-be litigants.

See *esto consentiens adversario*.

Alias 'otherwise'. In English it has come to mean 'otherwise called', referring to an adopted name.

Alibi 'elsewhere'. An accused who contends that he cannot be guilty of a crime charged, because he was somewhere else at the time of its commission, raises an *alibi* defence. Might this be changed to a '*not there*' defence?

See Preface.

Aliena negotia curo. Excussus propriis 'I attend to other people's affairs: baffled with my own'. Horace. Lawyers chide those who do not read the small print, but seldom read their own.

Alieni generis 'of another *or* different kind'.

Aliquando dormitat bonus Homerus 'even good Homer sometimes nods off'. Horace, *Ars Poetica,* 359. A judge should not be blamed for any slip or small error or even if he actually nods gently off to sleep. But perhaps if he snores.

Aliquot 'some, so many'. An *aliquot* part is one of so many. A known fraction and integral part of a whole.

Aliter 'otherwise'.

Allocatur 'it is allowed'. The certificate of a court officer showing that an amount certified is payable as taxed costs. Since by the CPR 'taxation' is now called 'detailed assessment', taxed costs will presumably be referred to as costs in respect of which a detailed assessment has been made.

Alma Mater 'nourishing mother'. The expression is used usually in relation to a person's school, college or university.

Alter ego 'other I *or* self'. An expression often used to refer to the same person in a different status, capacity or even personality. Also an inseparable companion.

Alumnus 'foster child' *or* 'nursling'. Used to describe a graduate or former student of a university or academic institution. The plural is *alumni*; the feminine is *alumna* and the feminine plural *alumnae*.

A mensa et t(h)oro 'from table and bed'. Used in relation to divorce, 'Divorce *a mensa et toro*' is a decree, order or official acknowledgement that living quarters will no longer be shared by one-time spouses.
See *a vinculo matrimonii.*

Amicus curiae 'friend of the court *or* tribunal'. One (a volunteer or invitee) who is not a party to proceedings, but who is permitted to take an active part in them so as to assist the court or tribunal with research, argument and submissions (as appropriate) usually in a case of difficulty where one interest is not represented but also where it is thought that an independent view may be valuable. This is sometimes particularly appropriate in the context of an adversarial system. The expression had been replaced by the English 'advocate to the court'. Yet on 9th May 2005 in the *Times* report of *Ward* v *Commisioner of Police of the Metropolis and Anor* an *amicus curiae* was named.

See *locus standi*.

Animo furandi 'with the intention of stealing'.

Animus 'intention, spirit *or* mind'. A manifestation of hostility or ill-feeling.

Animus possidendi 'intention to possess'. Used in relation to claims based upon adverse possession of land. See Slade J in *Powell* v *McFarlane* and anor. 1979 PP and CR 452, 'Against this background, it is not surprising that . . . the courts have been reluctant to infer the necessary *animus possidendi*'. See too Lord Hutton in *J.A. Pye (Oxford)* v *Graham* [2002] 3 WLR 221 at 245. The Land Registration Act 2002 (which does not have retrospective effect) enabled a squatter to apply to be registered as owner after ten years of adverse possession. The party otherwise entitled to immediate possession is then required to regularize the situation by evicting the squatter within two years in default of which the squatter is entitled to be registered with the title of that party. In *J.A. Pye (Oxford) Ltd and Anor* v *UK*. (Application No. 44302/02) the European Court of Human Rights on 23rd November 2005 held squatter's rights to be an unfair burden on landowners and a violation of Article 1 of Protocol No 1 (*Times*, 23rd November 2005).

Animus revertendi 'intention of turning back'.

Anno Domini 'in the year of the Lord'. Full version of the abbreviation AD. Western calendars calculate passage of time from the supposed birth of Christ. For practical purposes the commencement date is arbitrarily accepted, though there is disagreement as to the exact year of Christ's birth. Whilst AD is abbreviated from Latin, BC, is English-based: Before Christ.

The letters AD should always be placed before the number and the letters BC after the number.

Anno regni 'in the year of the reign'. Used in relation to the passage of years in a monarch's reign and in particular in the dating of statutes.

Ante cibum 'before food'. Words, often abbreviated to AC, to be found in medical notes or on prescriptions, denoting that something is to be administered or taken before food.

See *BD*, *nocte* and *post cibum*.

Ante meridiem 'before noon'. Full version of the abbreviation a.m.

A posteriori 'from what follows'. Proceeding from effects to causes. Empirical.

See *a priori*.

A priori 'from what comes before'. From what is already known. The expression is usually used in relation to reasoning. *A priori* reasoning is that whereby deductions are made from what went before, i.e., prior knowledge, actual or assumed.

Arbitrium boni 'the (common-sense) view of the good person'. Expression used by Slesser LJ in *Byrne* v *Deane* [1937] 1 KB at p. 833: 'We have to consider in this connection the *arbitrium boni*, the view which should be taken by the ordinary good and worthy subject of the King.' Analogous is the well-known criterion for determining what is reasonable in the field of negligence, namely the assumed view of the reasonable 'man in the street' or 'the man on the Clapham omnibus'. See Greer LJ in *Hall* v *Brooklands Auto-Racing Club* [1933] 1 KB 205 at p. 224. Less well known is the observation of Mr Justice Hilbery in *Lea* v *Justice of the Peace Ltd*, reported *sub nom* 'Privacy and the Press', London 1947 at p. 146: 'God forbid that the standard of manners should be taken from the man on the Clapham omnibus.'

Arcana imperii 'secrets of authority'. State secrets.

Ardentia verba 'vehement *or* glowing words'. Counsel's plea in mitigation. *Copia verborum* 'fluency of speech' would be an asset too.

See *blandae mendacia, deprehendi miserum, homines enim* and *rem tene*.

Assoilzie Not Latin; a word of Latin–French derivation belonging to Scots Law and so delightful that its omission in a work directed primarily to lawyers would be a shame. To be *assoilzied* is not to suffer an unthinkably dreadful fate. On the contrary *assoilzie* means to absolve or free a defender or an accused respectively from a claim or charge made against him.

Assumpsit 'he has taken upon him'. The old Common Law action of *assumpsit* alleged that a man had taken upon himself to do something which developed into obligation: the law of contract.

Audaces fortuna juvat 'fortune comes to the aid of the bold'.

Audi alteram partem 'hear the other side'. St Augustine of Hippo, *354–430, De Duabus Animabus XIV. 2*. A maxim denoting basic fairness and a canon of natural justice. A judge or adjudicator in disputes should allow both parties to be heard and should listen to the point of view or case of each.

Ave atque vale 'hail and farewell'. Catullus ci.10. Words written to the poet's deceased brother.

A vinculo matrimonii 'from the bond of marriage'. A divorce *a vinculo matrimonii* is the release from the obligations of that status. *Vinculum* may also mean chain.

See *a mensa et t(h)oro*.

B

BD Abbreviation of *bis die*: 'twice daily'. To be found in medical notes and on prescriptions, signifying that the dose of a medicine identified is to be given, or that some therapy is to be implemented, twice daily.

See *ante cibum* and *post cibum*.

Blandae mendacia linguae 'falsehoods of a smooth tongue'. Beware the silver tongued advocate.

An apocryphal story has it that a judge answered in dulcet tones the smooth and persuasive plea (not false) of counsel, that time already served in custody prior to trial was sufficient without more to meet the justice of the case, with quotation from Samuel Taylor Coleridge's 'Rime of the Ancient Mariner':

The other was a softer voice,
As soft as honey dew:
Quoth he, 'The man hath penance done,
And penance more will do'.

In a criminal case of certain authenticity, counsel in full and urgent flight, pleading in mitigation, stopped suddenly in his tracks.

'I see Your Honour smile. Do I infer that Your Honour is not with me?'

'You must not infer,' replied the Recorder, 'Such is the force of your eloquence that, when you have concluded, I shall have to retire for a little and think for myself, so as to ensure that I am not railroaded into incautious error.

See *ardentia verba* and *homines enim*.

Bona fide 'in good faith', genuinely, sincerely, honestly, without deception.

Bona fides 'good faith', an honest or sincere intention.

Bona vacantia 'goods without (an apparent or traceable) owner', to which the Crown is entitled, e.g., old shipwrecks and treasure trove. Where nobody entitled under the rules for intestacy can be traced, an intestate's estate belongs to the Crown, the Duchy of Lancaster or the Duke of Cornwall as appropriate.

See *res nullius*.

Boni viri arbitratus 'the decision of a fair man'.

See *aequo animo*.

Brevi manu 'with a short hand', summarily, off hand.

Brutum fulmen 'a senseless (stupid) thunderbolt'. From Pliny. Natural History II. Xliii. An empty threat. The expression was used by *Rix LJ in R (Williamson)* v *Secretary of State for Education and Employment* [2003] 1 AER 385 at p 434. 'This would ascribe to Parliament a complete *brutum fulmen*'.

C

CAV see *curia advisari vult*.

Cadit quaestio 'the question falls', the question is at an end. There will be no further discussion or argument. More disposed to kill rather than argue with those who opposed him, the young Octavian (later Emperor Augustus) perhaps exemplified the highwater mark of this expression.

Caesaris Caesari 'Caeser's things to Caesar'. A Latin shorthand denoting that rights or chattels go to those entitled. Probably based upon and abbreviated from *reddite ergo quae sunt caesaris* (below).

Cancellarius 'Chancellor'. The Lord Chancellor used to be a judge, the head of the judiciary, the Speaker of the House of

Lords, an unelected Cabinet Minister, a Privy Councillor and custodian of the Great Seal. As Speaker he sat upon the Woolsack and had done so from the reign of Edward III (1327—77) when it was symbolic of wool as the main source of the country's wealth. His position was one of immense power and corresponding responsibility. In the absence of a written constitution, he was entrusted with the delicate task of maintaining the separation of his executive and judicial powers (being the custodian of the judiciary's independence). He was also responsible for the administration of Royal Patronage hence recommendation for appointment by the Queen (the Monarch) of Judges and Queen's (King's) Counsel.

Something of the infallible prevailed in the autocratic 'accountable to none' practices which came to mark some behaviour of his Department. The last Lord Chancellor, Lord Irvine of Lairg, was moved to compare himself in terms of *imperium* (see below) with Cardinal Thomas Wolsey. Unlike Wolsey, however, he never aspired to become Pope.

The office of Lord Chancellor was, suddenly and without warning, purportedly abolished by a press announcement from Downing Street on 12th June 2003. It was to be succeeded by a new position, the Secretary of State for Constitutional Affairs which Lord Falconer of Thoroton was to occupy: heading a new Department for Constitutional Affairs.

More than a 'Prime Ministerial back of an envelope re-shuffle' was however necessary effectively and conveniently to abolish the ancient office of Lord Chancellor. Lord Falconer was nominated additionally as Lord Chancellor to carry out the functions of that office while the proposed changes were further considered and regularized. In February 2004 a Bill was published anticipating abolition of the office of Lord Chancellor. After much Parliamentary wrangling the outcome, following the passing of the Constitutional Reform Act 2005, is in summary: that the office of Lord Chancellor survives with modifications: that the holder of that office need not be a lawyer or a member of the House of Lords (hence will not be Speaker of the House of Lords): that he/she will sit in Cabinet and act as a bridge between the executive and the judiciary; but will no longer sit as a judge or be head of the judiciary. The latter position has passed to the Lord Chief Justice of England.

A Judicial Appointments Commission has now been set up and Queen's Counsel (after a period of doubt as to whether the position would survive following suspension in 2002) will be appointed through a selection panel assisted by an independent Secretariat. There will be *inter alia* self assessment, evidence from referees (specified judges and legal practitioners nominated by the applicant) and interview. There will be a charge of £1,800 (plus VAT!) on application and a further £2,250 levied against those appointed. The office may be taken away for cause but this does not apply to those already appointed. In 2005 there were 443 applicants under the new scheme. In July 2006, 175 of these were successful of whom 33 were women.

The new system can scarcely fail to be an improvement on the old, reliant as that was on secret files and secret soundings and breaching most canons of natural justice. The old system operated as a lottery in which justice was not seen to be done and was calculated to demoralize many of those rejected who in a system of patronage were left without explanation or recourse.

The Treason Act of 1351 (reign of Edward III) made it a capital offence to 'slay the Chancellor' but only when in his place doing his office. The death penalty for this offence remained until 27th January 1999, when the UK signed up to the relevant protocol of the European Convention on Human Rights, which did away with the death penalty in peacetime.

See *fiat justitia* and *in vino veritas*.

Capax doli 'capable of crime *or* fraud'. See *doli capax*. The opposite is *incapax doli*.

Capitis deminutio 'deterioration of status'. An expression of Roman law denoting broadly disadvantageous change of status.

Captator 'catcher, deceiver, grabber'. A person who obtains a gift or legacy through artifice.

Casus belli 'an opportunity of war'. A justification for war. Excuse for war.

Causa causans 'cause causing'. The real, proximate, immediate or main cause.

See *causa sine qua non*.

Causam obtinere 'to win one's cause *or* case.' A barrister is always anxious to say: '*causam meam obtinui*', 'I have won my case', particularly to his clerk. But, when he cannot, he need not worry too much. Sir Patrick Hastings wrote: 'I have known so many advocates, good advocates and very good advocates, bad advocates and very bad advocates, and in the result I am satisfied that at least ninety per cent of all cases win or lose themselves and that the ultimate result would have been the same whatever counsel the parties had chosen to represent them.' *Cases in Court* (Pan Books, 1953), p. 250. Those barristers, who may yet be permitted to advertise by reference to success rates, could be suspect, but in the remaining ten per cent or less, choice of counsel may be crucial. Sir Gavin Lightman, quoted speaking critically of the Queen's Counsel in *The Times* on 9th June, 1998, said:

> The quality of counsel undoubtedly does have an effect on a party's cause, and can have an effect on the outcome. That is why these fees (large fees to Queen's Counsel) are paid. It must be a matter of serious concern if leaders (QCs) of the first rank charge fees beyond the range reasonably affordable by ordinary litigants, but fees their wealthy and powerful opponents can afford. There is then no equality before the law. An imbalance in legal representation can work grave injustice. The judge will no doubt seek to maintain some form of balance, but there is a limit to what he is permitted to do. Where for example equality in skills of cross-examination is missing, or one side over-awes counsel for the other (as does on occasion happen) a tangible advantage is obtained and justice is tilted by pure purchasing power.

A story of Edward Carson QC (apocryphal perhaps) is demonstrative of how illustrious counsel may keep the boat afloat and even save the day. Addressing a three-judge court of appeal, he was interrupted by one: 'You have no case, Mr Carson:

this is unarguable'. Carson did not respond and carried right on. A little later the same judge repeated his view with distinct venom. Carson paused. 'I did hear and understand your Lordship's earlier, with respect premature, observation since which my submissions have been directed to your two brother judges.' Only a real heavy would dare to answer in such vein.

Counsel's gross incompetence may, however, sometimes work to a defendant's advantage. Where it has been demonstrated that counsel's incompetence or failure to perform his duties were of a fundamental nature, an appellate court should proceed with great care before concluding that, even without these failings, the jury's verdict would inevitably have been the same. See *Boodram* v *State of Trinidad and Tobago.* Judicial Committee of the Privy Council, *The Times,* 15th May 2001.

Yet in February of 2005 those who in 1996, after a 313-day trial, had been ordered to pay damages for libelling McDonald's were themselves awarded damages by the European Court of Human Rights against the UK (in proceedings to which McDonald's was not party). The original trial had been long and complex. McDonald's had been represented by an array of expensive and experienced lawyers. The defendants had acted in person with intermittent *pro bono* assistance from lawyers, especially in relation to the drafting of pleadings. Legal Aid had not been available to them in the case of libel. The European Court held that the absence of Legal Aid constituted a breach of Article 6.1.

Causa sine qua non 'cause without which not'. Fundamental, if sometimes remote, or distant cause of something. A man stops on the pavement to speak to one who causes him to move to a position by the kerb, where, after a little, he is struck by a car. The person who caused him to move to that position may be the cause without which not. Nobody, however, would realistically think of him as a cause of the misfortune.

See *causa causans* and *sine qua non.*

Caveat 'let him beware'. A warning or proviso.

Cave 'beware'. One who keeps '*cave*' keeps lookout: especially among small schoolchildren for teacher. There are those who in youth thought it was spelt KV, and had no idea what those letters stood for.

Caveat emptor 'let the buyer beware'. A reference to the necessity for a buyer to be wary when making a purchase. If the goods acquired turn out to be defective, not suitable or not the vendor's property, etc., he might have to resort to the inconvenience and expense of litigation and might or might not find that he has satisfactory remedies. Initial care may save a lot of heartache.

Subject to statutory exceptions a buyer must satisfy himself of the quality, condition, fitness for purpose, etc., of what he is buying. The seller is not responsible. Horace explains the need for *caveat emptor: laudat venales qui vult extrudere merces*, 'he praises his wares who wishes to press them upon others'.

See *res vendita*

Certiorari 'to be made certain'. One of the old prerogative writs (along with *prohibition* and *mandamus*). These became judicial orders issuing out of the Queen's Bench Division. *Prohibition* is a like order issued to prevent an inferior court from exceeding its jurisdiction or acting contrary to the rules of natural justice. *Certiorari* is issued (often along with *prohibition*) to review the actions of an inferior court (e.g., if it had acted *ultra vires*, 'in excess of its jurisdiction') and to quash its decision if appropriate. *Mandamus* (we command) is an order to carry out some public duty.

The Times of 19th July 2000, reported Lord Woolf, the Lord Chief Justice, as informing the American Bar Association that he was abolishing use of the court order known as *certiorari*. It has been replaced by a 'quashing order'. See Preface. Such an order would now be obtained upon an application for judicial review.

Statutory instrument 1033/2004 swept away the Latin names for the prerogative orders. *Mandamus*, prohibition and *certiorari* became respectively 'mandatory', 'prohibiting' and 'quashing orders'.

Certum est quia impossibile est 'It is certain because it is impossible'. Tertullian. *De carne christi* 5.

Certum est quod certum reddi potest 'something is certain if it is capable of being made certain'.

See Rix LJ in *Scammel and Anor* v *Dicker, The Times,* 27th April 2005.

Cessante ratione legis, cessat lex ipsa 'when the reason for a law ceases, the law itself ceases'. See the speech of Lord Hoffmann in *Arthur J.S. Hall and Co.* v *Simons* [2000] 3 WLR 543 p. 576.

Ceteris paribus 'other things being equal'.

Cf An abbreviation of *confer*, which means 'compare'.

Child See *minor*.

Circa 'about'. Denotes uncertainty; especially about a date. *Circa* 1900, around 1900. Usually abbreviated e.g., *c.* 1900.

Citius venit periculum cum contemnitur 'danger arises when it is despised'. Publilius Syrus. Those who take insufficient care, who are contemptuous of and ignore danger, are the most likely to come to grief. A useful phrase to bear in mind when considering liability for negligence, the degree of contributory negligence and *volenti non fit injuria.*

Clare constat 'it clearly is established'. A writ for succession to property.

Cognoscenti 'those who know'. Used to describe those with knowledge in the field, particularly art, music and literature. Though taken from the Latin (*cognoscere* 'to have knowledge of') this is an Italian not a Latin word.

Coitus 'going together', sexual intercourse.

Coitus interruptus 'interrupted sexual intercourse'. A use of Latin to describe discreetly and succinctly an unreliable form of contraception whereby intercourse is interrupted by withdrawal before ejaculation. Abolition of this expression in the Divorce Courts would be inconvenient. Edward Gibbon made the point in 1796: 'My English text is chaste, and all licentious passages are left in the obscurity of a learned language.' By obscurity, he later made clear, he meant 'decent obscurity' ... good taste? These passages are often in footnotes to be decoded by those who can and want to.

Commorientes 'those dying together'. Persons who die together or on the same occasion and where it cannot be ascertained which one died first. In such cases statutory presumptions are made by the Law of Property Act 1925 and the Intestate's Estates Act 1952 as to the sequence of death for purposes of the devolution of property.

Commune bonum 'a common good'.

Commune consensu 'by common consent'.

Communis error facit jus 'generalized error makes law'. Application by judges of what is erroneously believed to be the law will be the law (*de facto*) for the time being. Thus in the 42nd (and 43rd) edition of *Archbold Criminal Pleading, Evidence and Practice* (for 1985 and 1988 respectively) it is stated that 'upon an indictment for assault occasioning actual bodily harm (abh) the Defendant may be convicted of common assault'; and, at S20:120 is set out a form of indictment for abh and it is repeated that on this indictment a defendant might be convicted of (the lesser offence) of common assault. This was followed by judges and counsel alike for some considerable time until the case of *R* v *Mearns* [1991] QB 82 decided that this was not so. A person might not be convicted of common assault unless a specific count was included in or added to the indictment (effect of Sections 39 and 40 of the Criminal Justice Act 1988 and S. (3) of the Criminal Law Act 1967). A large number of consolidated appeals against conviction for common assault were allowed following this case but for a great many generalized error had made the law for years and it was too late for remedy.

Compos mentis 'possessed of mind', of sound mind, having control of mind, sane.
    See *non compos mentis*.

Concordat 'is of one mind'. Agreement. Particularly between the Roman Catholic Church and a state or secular government.

Consensus 'agreement'. A general agreement of opinion or testimony. A collective opinion.

Consilio et prudentia 'by counsel and prudence'.

Consortium 'a community *or* fellowship'. The same word is used in English but tends to be used in reference to those in association for a business purpose or venture, often to take over a company. The Latin plural, *consortia* (consortiums), is optional in English; likewise with *ultimatum*. On 29th June 2001, while giving evidence at the Old Bailey in the trial of Lord Archer for perverting the course of justice and for perjury, Lady Archer stated that she did not deliver *ultimata*.

Constat 'it is agreed'. *Constat inter omnes*, 'it is agreed among all'. *Non constat*, 'it is not agreed *or* is unclear'.

Contemporanea expositio est optima et fortissima in lege 'contemporary exposition is the best and strongest in law'. The best and surest way of construing a document is to read it in the sense in which it was applied when it was drawn up.

Contra 'against'. Before administering a drug with known side-effects on certain people, a doctor will look for *contra* indications in his patient.

Contra bonos mores 'contrary to good morals'. Used in the law to denote something contrary to the moral welfare of society. An agreement to commit a crime would be *contra bonos mores*. See e.g., *Bennett* v *Bennett* [1952] 1 KB 249 at pp. 253–4.

Contra mundum 'against the world'. Defying or opposing everyone. Against all comers. Two children who had tortured and murdered a third younger child were reported by *The Times* on 9th January 2001, as soon to be released from detention. No effort was to be spared by the Home Office to prevent their identification thereafter. In the High Court Dame Elizabeth Butler-Sloss made an order banning publication in the British media of any information related to their appearance, identity or whereabouts. The ban is permanent, said the *Times* leader and is made *contra mundum* to embrace the repetition of information already published by foreign media or on the Internet. Dame Elizabeth acknowledged that it was a significant extension of the law of confidence, being of general not just particular effect.

Contra pacem 'against the peace'. The concept of King's/Queen's Peace is that maintenance of law and order, and provision for justice generally, are matters for the Crown. So we have the Royal Courts of Justice and criminal prosecutions are brought by the Crown. In the laws of King Canute *circa* 1027 (written, not in Latin, but in Old English) breach of the King's Peace included housebreaking, ambush, receiving outlaws and neglect of summons to army service.

Any illegal violence is against the King's/Queen's Peace and charges for assault, etc., used to end with the words *contra pacem Domini nostri Regis*. An extract from Archbold, *Criminal Pleading, Evidence and Practice*, 38th edn (Sweet and Maxwell, 1973) (costing £15 then and £290 in 2005) at s. 3586 relates to the common-law offence of riotous assembly and assault and is noteworthy: 'it has even been held that, if a number of persons assemble for the purpose of abating a public nuisance, and appear with spades, iron crows and other tools for that purpose, and abate it accordingly without doing more, it is no riot. Dalt c. 137, unless threatening language or other misbehaviour, in apparent *disturbance of the peace*, be at the same time used.'

See *fons justitiae, justiciarius regni* and *regina*.

Contra proferentem 'against the (party) proferring'. A rule of interpretation. Where there is ambiguity or uncertainty in a document, it will be construed against the party proferring it, who is responsible for its content and must bear any adverse consequences flowing from its deficiencies. Ambiguity might be conveniently contrived but will not be advantageous if the document is, as the law requires, construed against the party responsible for it and in the way least favourable to him.

See *verba chartarum* and *omnia praesumuntur*.

Contra verbosos noli contendere verbis; sermo datur cunctis, animi sapientia paucis 'don't contend with words against wordy people; speech is given to all, wisdom to few'. Cato. What a prospectively useful courtroom quotation now denied to the judges.

Lawyers' verbosity is notorious. In *Gulliver's Travels* Jonathan Swift described lawyers as 'a society of men bred up from their youth in the art of proving by words multiplied for the purpose, that black is white and white is black according as they are paid'.

Lewis Carroll (Charles Dodgson) wrote in *Alice in Wonderland*:

> In my youth said the old man I took to the law
> And argued each case with my wife,
> And the muscular strength, which it gave to my jaw,
> Has lasted the rest of my life.

See *paucis verbis* and *rem tene verba sequentur*.

Coram judice 'in the presence of a judge'. After a court hearing a barrister will endorse the result on his brief, beginning with the word *Cor* (short for *coram*) followed by the name of the judge, e.g. '*Cor* Smith J. or 'Mr Justice Smith'.

A directive that barristers should abandon this practice and must endorse their briefs with 'in the presence of' (on pain of some taxation or detailed assessment penalty) may be expected.

Corpus delicti 'the body of the crime'. Originally referring to the corpse of a murdered person this expression has come to refer more generally to the factual apparent evidence of a crime.

Corpus juris 'the body of law'. The laws of a nation, state or city are its '*corpus juris*'. The *corpus juris civilis* is the civil law.

Corrigendum 'to be corrected', plural *corrigenda*. Errors to be corrected; usually spelling or printing.

See *erratum*.

Crassa negligentia 'gross negligence'.

Cui bono? 'to whom good?' Who stands to gain? Who will benefit? If looking for motive when trying to solve a crime, it may be useful to ask *cui bono*? Used by Cicero on numerous occasions, e.g., in *Pro Milone* 32.

Cui licitus est finis, etiam licent media 'where the end is lawful, the means too are lawful'. Jesuit maxim. Very dangerous!

Cuius est solum, ejus est usque ad caelum et usque ad inferos 'who owns the land owns it up to the sky and down to the depths'. A maxim relating to trespass to land and an owner or occupier's rights above and below the surface of the earth. State rights in relation to oil and the invasion of space make this very much a *prima facie* and simplistic statement in modern times. Note too: *Bernstein (Baron)* v *Skyviews Ltd* [1978] 1 QB 479.

Curia advisari vult 'the court wishes to be advised'. Abbreviated to CAV in law reports this indicates that judgement was reserved and given after consideration. It was not given *ex tempore* (see below). These letters appear, e.g., in *Bernstein (Baron)* v *Skyviews Ltd* [1978] 1 QB 479.

D

Damnum sine injuria esse potest 'there can be damage (in the sense both of physical injury or other consequential pecuniary loss) without injury (legal wrong)'. A plaintiff (claimant), who has suffered damage in consequence of the act of another, may not be entitled to recover compensation because the defendant's act was not in law wrongful, e.g., most injuries caused wholly accidentally in contact sports like rugby or damage done by way of competition in trade.
See *ubi jus ibi remedium* and *volenti non fit injuria*.

De bene esse 'concerning well being'. There is no satisfactory translation. The expression is of mysterious origin, much used notwithstanding; particularly by lawyers. Views differ as to its meaning. 'Provisionally' or 'for what it is worth' are the front runners (one barrister thought it meant 'for the purposes of argument'; others suggested 'for the hell of it' and 'let's get on with it'): often these come to much the same thing, e.g., if counsel, unable to prove a document until the arrival of a witness next day, were to put it before the judge *de bene esse*, that might be said to be 'provisionally', but in a longer term sense, if the necessary probative witness were to die, it might also be said to be 'for what it is worth'. The expression is used, therefore, sometimes to propose a course not strictly permissible but convenient, sensible and/or the best possible in the circumstances, e.g., on application for a retrial based upon a document not originally introduced in evidence, asking the appeal court to look at the document *de bene esse*. It is known to be very effective if acceded to in cases where, once the document was seen, it seemed wrong to deny a retrial on technical legal grounds.

It is remarkable that an expression, the exact meaning of which is uncertain, should have come to be so widely used in a profession renowned for being pedantic (understandably, as its members struggle eternally for certainty in what is the most inexact of sciences). One learned authority (Barry Nicholas, see preface) admitted to having no idea as to what it meant and, for that reason, said that it was an expression which he had never used.

In Lord Lane's earlier days, when sitting as Chairman of Quarter Sessions, he was faced with counsel, who put forward a document stated to be *de bene esse*. 'What exactly does that mean?' asked the Chairman. Counsel, in distress, took refuge in much verbiage. 'I see,' said the Chairman at last. 'Latin must be a wonderful language if it can say all that in three words.'

There is a further story, apocryphal perhaps and not strictly *ad rem* (see above), of the same Chairman after he had become Lord Chief Justice. He had a brush with a lorry, stopped, got out of his car and was surprised to hear the suggestion that it was his fault. 'We had better go by the book,' he said, noting the lorry's index number and asking for name, address, etc. 'By the bleedin' book,' said the lorry driver, 'Mr High and Mighty. S'pose you think you're the Lord Chief bleedin' Justice?' 'It so happens that I am.'

De bonis asportatis 'concerning goods taken away'. Originally the name given to one form of a writ of trespass: later the name given to conversion.

Decretum 'a decree' (plural *decreta*). Directives emanating from Brussels are *decreta*.

De die in diem 'from day to day'. When an injury is continuing (e.g., a nuisance) a new cause of action accrues *de die in diem*. May be important in relation to limitation.

De facto . . . de jure 'from *or* by the fact . . . from *or* by the law.' A government may rule in reality and fact, even though it has no legal or constitutional right to do so. It is a *de facto* government, not a *de jure* government.

De jure See *de facto*.

Delegatus non potest delegare 'one to whom something is delegated cannot (further) delegate'. In *Barnard* v *National Dock Labour Board* [1953] 2 QB 18, delegation of the Board's disciplinary powers to a port manager without statutory authority was unacceptable while in *Carltona* v *Commissioner of Works* [1943] 2 All ER 560, delegation to an official in a government department was tolerated, even though the powers had been given to the Minister only. The strict maxim appears to be flexible in practice. An area of law to be researched and considered with care.

Delictum 'a wrongful act, fault *or* (sometimes) crime'.

De minimis non curat lex 'the law does not concern itself with the smallest things *or* trifles'. Some matters are of such minimal significance that the law will not involve itself with them. Bacon Letter CCLXXXii.

De mortuis nil (nihil) nisi bonum 'concerning the dead nothing unless it be good'. Don't speak ill of the dead. In deference perhaps to *audi alteram partem* (see above): they are not here to be heard and defend themselves. There is generally however no need to speak ill of the dead because:

> The evil that men do lives after them;
> The good is oft interréd with their bones;
> So let it be with Caesar.

> Mark Antony in William Shakespeare's *Julius Caesar*,
> Act III Sc. 2.

De novo 'anew'. To start all over again may be expressed shortly by use of this expression. Start *de novo*.

Deo gratias 'thanks be to God'.

Deo volente 'God willing'. Abbreviated to DV. I will see you next year *deo volente*, i.e., all being well or provided I am still alive.

Deprehendi miserum est 'it's wretched to be caught'. Horace, *Satires* 1:ii:134. Expression to be used in mitigation by erudite counsel.
  See *ardentia verba*.

Deus ex machina 'god from a machine'. A providential intervention or solution, just in time. The explanation of this meaning, apparently unrelated to the Latin, is that in the Greek theatre it was not unusual for a god to be introduced to 'sort things out'. His arrival on the scene was from above and was effected by mechanical means.

Deus vult 'God wills it'.

Devastavit 'he has laid waste'. Used in relation to trustees or personal representatives. If loss is attributable to neglect on the part of such persons they are said to have committed a *devastavit*.

Dextra manu 'with the right hand'.
See *sinistra manu.*

Dicta See *obiter dictum.*

Dictum See *obiter dictum.*

Dictum factum 'said, done', no sooner said than done.

Dimidium facti qui coepit habet: sapere aude 'to have begun is half the battle: be sensible and bold'. Horace, *Ars Poetica* 40. Don't put off prospectively difficult or disagreeable tasks. Lawyers should not become part of the law's delays and should immediately address their 'too difficult pile' of pending matters. Easier said than done!

Discite justitiam moniti 'be warned and learn justice'. Description written above entrance to the old Courts in the Town Hall of Oxford.

Dissentiente 'dissenting'.

Doli capax 'capable (legally) of wrong *or* fraud'. A child under the age of ten is not deemed capable of committing a crime (is *doli incapax).* See *capax doli.*

Dolus 'fraud' or bad faith'.

Domus sua cuique est tutissimum refugium 'to each person his home is the safest refuge', preceded by 'for a man's house is his castle', this famous phrase (elsewhere: 'the house of everyone is to him as his castle and fortress') is from the third part of Sir Edward Coke's *Institutes of the Laws of England.*
    Coke was prosecuting counsel at Sir Walter Raleigh's trial held in Winchester (on account of an outbreak of plague in London) for treason in 1603. His conduct of the prosecution was 'the most scandalous of all the series of 17th century State Trials'. See Stephen, *History of the Criminal Law*, vol. 1, p. 333. He became Chief Justice of the Common Pleas in 1606 and later of

the King's Bench. He developed an intense reverence for the common law and is possibly the greatest figure in its history. Fearlessly he resisted the prerogative claims of King James I. The Lord Chancellor, Lord Ellesmere (as Sir Thomas Egerton, responsible in earlier times for settling the indictment for that travesty of a trial of Mary, Queen of Scots; the brief for her prosecution is still in the possession of the Inner Temple), was instrumental in securing his dismissal by the King in 1616. Lord Ellesmere's portrait hangs in Brasenose College, Oxford.

See *durante beneplacito*.

Dona clandestina sunt semper suspiciosa 'secret gifts are always suspicious'. In modern times such gifts seem usually to involve brown envelopes.

Dubitante 'doubting'.

Dum casta vixerit 'so long as she shall have lived chastely'.

Dum sola 'while single' i.e. unmarried (of women).

Durante beneplacito 'while it well pleases'. In the reigns of James I and Charles I judges held office *durante beneplacito*, 'so long as it well pleases' (the King). After Charles's defeat in the Civil War, the judges' patent was changed to make their continued tenure depend upon their good behaviour *quamdiu se bene gesserint*, 'so long as they shall have behaved well'. In 1668, however, Charles II reinstated appointment *durante beneplacito*. James II in turn made free use of his power of summary dismissal in order to ensure support for his extreme prerogative claims, and made convenient judicial appointments with little regard to ability. At the trial of the seven bishops in 1688, the Court of King's Bench comprised four nondescript lawyers, two of whom were of infamous character. Among those appearing for the bishops were eminent lawyers, some of whom were former judges, who had been dismissed from office. Radcliffe and Cross, *The English Legal System*, 3rd edn. (Butterworth, 1954), p. 338. James had ordered his second Declaration of Indulgence to be read in the churches. Seven bishops, headed by the Primate, William Sancroft, protested against this use of the dispensing power. The clergy obeyed their superiors and the declaration went unread. Infuriated by this defiance, the King insisted that the bishops be put on trial for seditious libel. Refusing the bail proffered, the bishops were committed to the Tower before ultimately being found not guilty. By the Act of Settlement 1701 the tenure of judicial office was laid down as *quamdiu se bene gesserint*. Judges were to be removable by the King only upon an address of both Houses of Parliament. High Court Judges and above still hold office on this basis until their compulsory retirement at the age of seventy.

E

E converso 'conversely'.

E curia 'from the court'.

E.g. See *exempli gratia*.

Ejusdem generis 'of the same type'. A rule of construction and interpretation of documents and statutes. Closely associated with *noscitur a sociis* (see below). Where particular words describing a genus or category of persons or things are followed by general words, then (subject to any specific contra-indication) the general words will be confined to persons or things of the same class as the particular words.

Entia non sunt multiplicanda praeter necessitatem 'things are not to be enlarged (proliferated) more than is necessary'. Attributed to William Occam *circa* 1280–1349. An expression associated with 'Occam's Razor' which relates to the cutting out of superfluous material: terminology favoured by at least one member of the judiciary when faced with cases involving legion issues and mountainous documentation. Most counsel are bewildered, have to go and look the expression up, and then discover the explanatory Latin.

Ergo 'therefore'.

Erratum 'an error'. An error in writing or printing. The plural, *errata*, is often used in a list of corrected errors attached to a book etc.
   See *corrigendum*.

Est aliquid quod non oporteat etiamsi licet 'there is something which is not fitting (which one should not do) even if it is lawful', Cicero. Seneca puts it thus: *laus est facere quod decet non quod licet* 'it is praiseworthy to do what one ought to do not (only) what one is permitted (by law) to do'. Some things just won't do. Tax lawyers and accountants spend much of their time dissecting the law with a view to determining just how much tax their client can lawfully avoid; and avoid often comes close to evade.
   See *qui et idoneos*.

Esto consentiens adversario tuo cito dum es in via cum eo: ne forte tradat te adversarius judici, et judex tradat te ministro: et in carcerem mittaris 'be at agreement with thy adversary quickly, whilst thou art in the way [still on speaking terms] with him: lest perhaps the adversary deliver thee to the judge, and the judge deliver thee to the officer and thou be cast into prison'. Vulgate. St Matthew, ch. 5 v. 25. Neither the hazard of litigation nor the cost of proceedings must ever be underestimated. Amicable compromise early on is invariably the prudent policy. Plautus observed: *nescis tu quam meticulosa res sit ire ad judicem . . .* you don't know what a terrible thing it is to go to the judge (law).
   See *quid faciam*.

Et al 'and others', abbreviation of *et alii, et aliae, et alia*, the masculine, feminine and neuter forms respectively.

Et cetera 'and other things', the rest, abbreviated to *etc.*

Exacta diligentia 'with precise diligence *or* with appropriate prudence'.

Ex abundanti cautela 'from an abundance of care'. One might wear two watches or a belt in addition to braces *ex abundanti cautela.*

Ex adverso 'from the opposite side'. From the enemy, my learned friend!
See *fas est ab hoste doceri.*

Ex aequo et bono 'from what is equal and good', equitably, according to what is just and good; judicial objective.

Excelsior 'higher, more exulted'. *Excelse* means 'loftily'. Judges should beware lest they behave loftily. It may help if they were to avoid the expressions: 'I am much obliged, it matters not, beyond peradventure, not one jot or tittle, abundantly clear, so be it and there is not one *scintilla* of evidence'. They should take care too not to think in the words of W.S. Gilbert in *The Yeomen of The Guard*:

> For now I am a judge
> And a good judge too,
> And a good job too.

Until the House of Lords is reached there are always higher courts capable of inflicting humiliation so that *verecundus* (modesty) is a good Latin word with which to be familiar.
See *gravitas* and *scintilla.*

Exceptio probat regulam 'the exception proves the rule'. There can be an exception only if there is a rule.

Excerpta 'extracts'.

Ex contractu 'from the contract'. Liability is *ex contractu,* 'contractual'.

Ex debito justitiae 'out of the obligation of justice'. A remedy which an applicant gets as of right. The court is bound to give it: there is no discretion to refuse. See e.g., *Nelson* v *Greening* *and Sykes* (Builders) Ltd, 26th Feb 2004, CA ref A3/2003/2608 per Chadwick LJ: 'a person who is affected by an order which can properly be described as a nullity is entitled as of right – or *ex debito justitiae* as it used to be put – to have the order set aside'.

Ex dolo malo non oritur actio 'a right of action does not arise from fraud'.
    See too: *ex turpi causa non oritur actio*.

Executor 'one who carries something out'. A person appointed by a testator to carry out the terms of his will.

Exempli gratia 'by the help of example', abbreviated to e.g., used in English to introduce an example. If a ban on use of Latin in the law is to be strictly observed, the abbreviation e.g., will have to give way to something like f.i. (for instance).
    See *id est*.

Ex gratia 'from favour'. As a favour and not from obligation. A payment is often made *ex gratia* to conclude a dispute but, at the same time, to make clear that liability is denied and to avoid payment of any costs.

Ex hypothesi 'from the hypothesis' (proposed).

Ex improviso 'out of or from the unforeseen'. '. . . if any matter arises *ex improviso*, which the Crown could not forsee, supposing it to be entirely new matter, which they may be able to answer only by contradictory evidence, they may give evidence in reply'. Per *Tindal CJ in R* v *Frost* [1839] 9 C and P 129. Subject to judge's discretion. For the *ex improviso* principle see Archbold, *Criminal Pleading, Evidence and Practice*, 2005 @ S 4-430–342.

Ex officio 'from one's office', by virtue of one's office or status. On account of a person's office or status he may be entitled to sit on a committee or be afforded some other privilege, favour or position.

Ex parte 'from a party *or* faction', from one side only. An application to the court by one party (or side), without the presence of the other, is *ex parte*. It was possible to have an *ex parte* application on notice. By the CPR an *ex parte* application is now named 'without notice' (but this does not quite replace like with like). How far this, without more, advances the man in the street's comprehension is questionable. These words also mean 'on behalf of' and are used in the title of case reports, e.g., *Regina* v *Bow Street Metropolitan Stipendiary Magistrate ex parte Pinochet Ugarte* [2000] 1 AC 61.

The proceeds of crime act 2002 is quite impartial. S 246(3) refers to an application to be made 'without notice'. S 42(1)(6), however, speaks of the court's power to make a restraint order on *ex parte* application in chambers. Since the Latin *ex parte* does not appear in the CPR and since elsewhere 'without notice' is used for the same thing, the definition section in the Act ought perhaps to have explained the expression and/or translated it.

See *nemo judex in causa sua*.

Ex post facto 'from what is done after'.

Expressio unius est exclusio alterius 'the expression of the one is the exclusion of the other'. A rule of construction and interpretation of deeds and statutes. The express mention in a document of one or more members or things of a particular class may be taken as tacitly excluding others of the same class which are not mentioned.

Expressum facit cessare tacitum 'what is expressly made (provided for) excludes what is tacit'. A rule of interpretation and construction of documents and statutes. Express mention of a person or thing excludes a person or thing of the same class not mentioned. The parties are deemed to have set out all they require.

Extant 'they are standing out'. The following matters are '*extant*', outstanding or still to be dealt with. A document still existing or surviving is *extant*.

Ex tempore 'from *or* out of time', extemporaneously, on the spur of the moment, unpremeditated. To speak *ex tempore* is to speak off the cuff, without preparation. A judgement given at the end of a case without time reserved is given *ex tempore*.

Ex turpi causa non oritur actio 'from a base cause *or* matter an action (potential remedy) does not arise'. The law does not assist in promoting underhand enterprises. 'No court ought to enforce an illegal contract or allow itself to be made the instrument of enforcing obligations alleged to arise out of a contract which is illegal, if the illegality is duly brought to the notice of the court, and the person invoking the aid of the court is himself implicated in the illegality.' Lindley LJ in *Gordon* v *Metropolitan Police Commissioner* [1910] 2 KB 1080 at p. 1098. See too *Kirkham* v *Chief Constable of Manchester* [1990] 2 QB 283 per Lloyd LJ. at p. 289. 'I come now to the two defences which lie at the heart of his appeal. They are expressed, for convenience, in the two Latin maxims *volenti non fit injuria* and *ex turpi causa non oritur actio.*'

The law as encapsulated in this maxim may also be invoked in tort. See *Pitts* v *Hunt* [1991] 1 QB 24. See too *ex dolo malo*.

Since the CPR the maxim must not be used in pleadings, as was common practice. Bullen and Leake and Jacob's *Precedents of Pleadings*, 15th edn. (Sweet and Maxwell, 2004) continues to retain the Latin as a useful label but does not include it in specimen pleading. See 71-S31 in vol. 2, p. 1183. Instead of a defence pleading: 'the Defendant will rely upon *ex turpi causa*' it will be necessary to include some long-winded assertion in English, e.g., 'The plaintiff (claimant) is not entitled to maintain a claim based upon matters which are unlawful and/or disreputable.'

Ex voto 'from a prayer or vow'. There are those judges who might leave some advocates in the dark with an observation such as: 'Your plea asks me optimistically, as it were *ex voto*, to take an unrealistically lenient course with your client.

F

Fac simile 'make *or* do like', an exact copy, facsimile.

Falsa demonstratio non nocet (cum de corpore constat) 'a false description does not harm (does not void or vitiate a document), when the body *or* main part is agreed, is clear'. A rule of construction and interpretation of documents and statutes.

Falsus in uno, falsus in omnibus 'false in one matter, false in all'. A *non sequitur* (see below), but a phrase sometimes reflected in advocates' cross-examination technique: occasionally unfair. Ask the witness if he is a truthful man (he of course answers 'yes') and remind him of the oath he swore, to tell the truth, the whole truth and nothing but the truth. Find and put to him a few *minutiae* (see below) in his evidence, which he has to admit were not true; then, in the context of as many admitted falsehoods as can be extracted, put to him what is said against him and, when inevitably he denies it, suggest to him that yet again he does not tell the truth.

Fas est ab hoste doceri 'it is right to be taught even by (learn even from) an enemy'. Ovid, *Metamorphoses* iv. 428. In the adversarial system of the courts in England and Wales the advocate regularly learns from an illustrious or fashionable opponent, his enemy (his learned friend!), to his client's cost but to his long-term gain and that of subsequent clients. This is called getting experience.
    See *a bove majori*.

Fellatio 'a sucking', sucking of the penis. Something which may aggravate a sexual offence so as to bear upon sentence. See *Regina* v *Willis* [1974] 60 Cr App R 146 at p. 149 (a sentencing guideline case) where, when considering emotional distress and indecent assault on boys, it was stated in the Court of Appeal that 'In some the assault may take the form of a revolting act of *fellatio*, which is as bad as buggery, maybe more so'.

Felo de se 'felon concerning himself'. One who commits suicide. A suicide. *Felo* is French mediaeval Latin of unknown origin. Following review of procedures relating to powers of coroners and death certification by a team set up after conviction of Harold Shipman (the serial killer doctor) it was proposed on 30th August 2002 that the expression 'death by own actions' should replace the word 'suicide' so that the stigma attaching to that word should be removed. Suicide was the intentional killing of oneself, and, until the Suicide Act of 1961, was a serious crime: self murder with the awful consequence that a failed attempt meant prosecution. 'Suicide' as a possible verdict for coroners' juries however remained and often involved detailed and protracted investigation of the intent of the deceased, distressing to relatives. The proposed terminology would include the *cri de coeur* which went wrong and would remove any issue as to the deceased's real intent to kill himself.

Ferae naturae 'untamed, wild by nature' (of an animal). Liability in the law of tort at Common Law in respect of damage caused by animals used to be related to whether they were of a species *ferae naturae* or *mansuetae naturae*, 'tame or gentle by nature', domesticated. Under the Animals Act 1971 the fundamentals are not much changed but the Latin terminology is superseded by reference to animals which are or are not of a dangerous species. See *scienter*.

Festina lente 'hurry slowly'. More haste less speed. Greek proverb quoted by Augustus, *Suetonius* xxv 4. Applicable to most undertakings but in particular to be heeded by retired gardeners over a certain age. Too fierce an attack on the overwhelming growth of weeds will almost certainly lead to painful dysfunction of some ageing limb and will set the whole project back,

Fiat 'let it be done', an authorization or go-ahead. The prosecution of certain offences requires the Attorney-General's *fiat*.

Fiat justitia (ruat caelum) 'let justice be done'. Sometimes is added *ruat caelum*, 'though the heavens fall'. Whatever the consequences, the doing of justice is paramount. In the early

1990s the Lord Chancellor's Department received from a disenchanted barrister an application for silk (to be made Queen's Counsel) stating *fiat justitia* and with the date in Roman numerals. The exhortation (for reasons of non-comprehension of the Latin or of the substantive concept or from outrage or other will never be known – all was jealously guarded secrecy) was not acceded to. *Ex abundanti cautela* (see above) the applicant omitted the addendum: *fieri facias* (see below).

Fiat justitia was for many years the motto of the General Council of the Bar – to be seen inscribed around a scales of justice logo. During the chairmanship of Mr Dan Brennan QC (later Lord Brennan) in December 1999 the Latin was superseded by English: 'justice for all'. The Latin was thought to be out of date and not user friendly. Surrender to political correctness?

See *cancellarius* and *in vino veritas*.

Fieri facias 'make or see it to be done', see to it. A writ of *fieri facias* (abbreviated usually to *fi. fa.*) was issued to enforce a judgement or order for the payment to, or for the recovery by, any person of money or costs. The writ was expressed in the general form of a royal direction to the sheriff of the county in which the goods of the debtor are situated, to seize in execution such goods of the debtor within that county as might be sufficient to satisfy the judgement debt. This expression survives the CPR: quite why is not apparent. See *nulla bona*.

Filius nullius 'nobody's son'.

Finis litium 'an end to dispute or litigation'. See *interest reipublicae*.

Fons justitiae 'fountain of justice'. The sovereign is the fountain of justice. Following collapse on 1st November 2002 of the prosecution case in *R* v *Burrell* (in which the former butler to Diana, Princess of Wales, had been accused of misappropriating some of her possessions) consequential upon information provided at a late stage by HM the Queen, there was complaint. It was contended that she should have spoken out earlier; the trial was said to have cost £1.5 million. There were calls for the abolition of the monarch's position as *fons justitiae* so as to make her liable to prosecution and to be obliged to give evidence in court. Suggestions were made that the wasted cost of the trial should be paid from the royal purse. See *contra pacem, justiciarius regni* and *regina*.

Fortescue, De Laudibus Legum Anglie (sic **Angliae**?) 'Fortescue, In praise of English laws'. Title of a book printed for and sold by John Amery 'at the Peacock near St. Dunstan's Church in Fleetstreet' in 1674. One of a number of books advertised in the *Compleat Lawyer*. Other books offered included Coke's *Commentary upon Littleton* 1670 and a *Liber Plasitandi* a book of special pleadings containing precedents, price 12 shillings (60p if comparison can be made). See *quicquid agas*.

Fortiter in re, suaviter in modo 'strong (resolute) in deed, gentle in manner'. How a judge should be. Used (the other way round, *suaviter in modo, fortiter in re*) of the law lord, Lord Salmon of Sandwich, in his obituary published by the *Daily Telegraph* on 9th November 1991.

Lord Chesterfield (1694–1773) said of these words: 'I do not know any one rule so unexceptionally useful and necessary in any part of life.'

Forum conveniens 'convenient *or* appropriate forum'. In deciding whether to permit service of proceedings out of the jurisdiction, the court has a discretion and will consider whether the English or foreign courts are the appropriate tribunal, the *forum conveniens*. The test is whether the interests of justice are best served by proceedings here or abroad.

In the case of Member States of the European Community note the Brussels Convention on Jurisdiction and Enforcement of Judgements in Civil and Commercial Matters 1968. See e.g., Cheshire and North, *Private International Law*, 13th edn (Butterworth) at p. 182 *et seq*.

Forum non conveniens 'a forum which is not convenient or appropriate'. The English courts will sometimes stay an action in England if the English Courts are not an appropriate or convenient forum. In *Spiliada Maritime Corporation* v *Cansulex Ltd,*

The Spiliada [1987] AC 460 at p. 476, Lord Goff of Chieveley said: 'The basic principle is that a stay will only be granted on the ground of *forum non conveniens* where the court is satisfied that there is some other available forum, having jurisdiction, which is the appropriate forum for trial of the action, i.e., in which the case may be tried more suitably for the interests of all the parties and the ends of justice.' See Cheshire and North's *Private International Law*, 13th edn (Butterworth) at p. 334 *et seq*.

See *lis alibi pendens*.

Freezing order see *Mareva*.

Fructus industriales 'industrial fruits', those resulting from man's labour or endeavour. Corn and other growths of the earth produced, not spontaneously, but by labour and industry. These have been regarded as goods as opposed to realty.

See *fructus naturales*.

Fructus naturales 'natural fruits'. The spontaneous product of the soil such as grass. *Prima facie* (see below) these adhere to the realty so as to be part of the land. Glanville Williams (Professor) in his book, *Learning the Law*, records these words as having been translated by one student as 'illegitimate children'. See *fructus industriales*.

Functus officio 'having performed *or* discharged his office'. No longer vested with the powers of office. Once a judgement is delivered and drawn up, a judge is *functus officio*. He has no power to alter his decision, which can be questioned only on appeal by others sitting in the Appeal Court.

G

Gaius Roman jurist (thought to have been a teacher of law) writing in the reign of Antoninus Pius (AD 138–61), source of much of our modern knowledge of Roman Law. His Institutes form the basis of Justinian's Institutes; the text is published with commentary and translation by F. de Zulueta. A restoration of Roman law in Oxford and a compulsory 'Roman Introduction to Private Law' paper at the preliminary jurisprudence examination (Moderations) will involve study of Gaius, albeit in translation. Latin not required. See *justitia est* and *summa itaque*.

Generalia 'general matters *or* principles'.

Generalia specialibus non derogant 'general provisions (in a statute) cannot derogate from specific provisions (in the same or another statute)'. A rule of statutory interpretation.

Gradatim 'step by step'. By degrees. This word may provide a judicial litmus test in respect of future Latin usage in the courts. Counsel might say to the judge: 'My Lord I fear that my argument does not appeal but may just not be understood. May I start again and take it *gradatim*? One judge might reply: 'Certainly, I am open minded and paid to sit and listen.' Another might say: 'Your argument makes me none the wiser. Must it really be repeated? In any event I do not understand the last word. If it be Latin, as I suspect, please use English in my court.' Bold counsel might respond: 'No wiser perhaps, but better informed?' (response courtesy of F. E. Smith, later Lord Birkenhead). The judge's indirect reference to Latin with distaste typifies esoteric judicial language or court jargon. 'I can't see you' means 'you are not properly dressed for court', e.g., a coloured collar is being worn or a single-breasted suit without a waistcoat. Equally, 'I hear what you say' means: 'I do not accept what is being said', and usually suggests that saying more will make no difference: an oblique form of 'shut up'.

Gratis 'by favour' (contraction of *Gratiis*). For nothing: without payment.

Gravitas 'solemn or dignified demeanour'. 'He lacks gravitas; they'll never make him a judge'.

Guardian ad litem see *litem* below.

H

Habeas corpus 'you are to have (produce) the body'. The name of a writ requiring a person to be brought before a judge or into court especially to determine the lawfulness of his or her detention. Based on the common law as declared in *Magna Carta* and the statutes which affirm it, this is a right available to any prisoner or person on his behalf directed to another who is detaining him, ordering production of the prisoner's body and treatment of it according as the court shall direct.

The right to apply for *habeas corpus* is denied by provisions contained in the Anti-Terrorism Crime and Security Act 2001 and inroads into the protection from arbitrary arrest and detention of the citizen are made by the European arrest warrant and surrender procedures of the member states of the EU and by the extended provisions for extradition at the request of the USA under the Extradition Act 2003. This Act is troubling. Designed to expedite the handing over of terrorist suspects, it does not require the US authorities to make a *prima facie* case. Sufficient is a statement of the case they hope to make out. On this questionable basis British subjects may be handed over to US justice. Further there is no reciprocity. Extradition of US citizens may not be demanded in the same way: the UK authorities must show evidence that an extraditable offence has been committed. In times past it was mandatory for a committing magistrate to inform a 'fugitive' that he had a right to apply for *habeas corpus* and that he would not be surrendered for 15 days so that such application could be made. See *judicium parium, nulli vendemus, nullus liber homo, satius est impunitum* and *Magna Carta*.

Habendum 'what is to be held'. The clause in a conveyance, which indicates the estate to be taken by the grantee.

Habendum et tenendum 'to have and to hold'.

Heu, modo itera omnia quae mihi nunc nuper narravisti, sed nunc Anglice? 'listen, would you repeat everything you have just told me, but this time say it in English? – from *Lingua Latina occasionibus omnibus* by Henry Beard. See *advocato suasus*.

His non obstantibus 'notwithstanding these things'.

Hoc sensu 'in this sense'.

Homines enim ad deos nulla re propius accedunt quam salutem hominibus dando 'for in nothing do men come closer to divinity than in granting deliverance to their fellow men'. Cicero, *Pro Ligario* 38.

Quintus Ligarius was prosecuted for bearing arms against Caesar and Cicero had undertaken his defence. Caesar (contravening a fundamental of natural justice, that no man should be judge in his own case, *nemo iudex in causa sua*) appointed himself judge. Worse still, Plutarch tells us, in advance of trial Caesar had declared: 'Why may we not give ourselves a pleasure which we have not enjoyed for so long, that of hearing Cicero speak; since I have already decided about Ligarius, who is plainly a bad man as well as being my enemy'.

Cicero's speech (effectively mitigation on a plea of guilty) before Caesar in the Forum was a masterpiece of forensic advocacy, perfection in construction, delivery and content. Towards the end he leaned on Caesar with the above quoted words. Caesar was overwhelmed. He became agitated and was visibly moved before letting some papers fall from his hand and discharging Ligarius. Few lawyers can have taken on such an unpromising case and emerged with such dazzling success. Ligarius repaid the compliment by joining Caesar's assassins. Would that Cicero had defended the admirable Vercingetorix.

Did Shakespeare borrow from Cicero when he wrote:

And earthly power doth then show likest God's
When mercy seasons justice.
The Merchant of Venice, Act IV, Scene i.

Useful material for today's advocate to quote when pleading in mitigation. He should however take care to check up upon his judge so as to know whether the Latin of Cicero or the English of Shakespeare is likely to be the more acceptable. This episode shows that no case is ever utterly without hope.

See *ardentia verba* and *nil desperandum*!

Honorarium Fee paid voluntarily, usually to a professional man, for services.

Hostis humani generis 'enemy of mankind', as such, in international law, a pirate is subject to capture, trial and imprisonment by all states. He automatically loses the protection of his flag state.

I

Ibid. Abbreviation of *ibidem*, 'in the same place'. Used by reference and text books in footnotes referring to an identical source cited in a preceding footnote.

Idem 'the same'. See *ad idem*.

Id est 'that is (to say)'. If the ban on Latin's use in the law is to be strictly enforced, the abbreviation of i.e., following the translation, will become 'tits'.

Ignorantia juris (legis) neminem excusat 'ignorance of the law excuses nobody'. It does not help the law-breaker that he did not know that what he did was an offence. 'Ignorance of the law excuses no man; not that all men know the law, but because 'tis an excuse every man will plead, and no man can tell how to refute him.' John Selden.

See *salus populi suprema lex esto*.

Progressively this understandable rule becomes potentially

productive of injustice as more and more delegated legislation passes through Parliament. One aspect of the rule of law is that the citizen should have access to and be able to determine the laws by which he is governed, so as to be able lawfully to order his life in society. Increasingly, however, empowering provisions are enacted under which regulations may be made. Lengthy and unreadable regulations are frequently drawn up, breach of which carries penalty. These are never considered by Parliament and are often known only to some official charged with overseeing the area in which the regulations apply. Most important, it is often a matter of difficulty to find out exactly when any such regulations came into force: often on such day as a minister shall appoint. But note the Statutory Instruments Act 1946 for some slight relaxation of this maxim; and access to legislative information available through the Internet has eased the problem. The law can be uncertain enough at the best of times: something acknowledged by Lord Hodson in *Boys* v *Chaplin* [1969] 3 WLR at p. 331. 'Rules of law should be defined and adhered to as closely as possible lest they lose themselves in a field of judicial discretion where no secure foothold is to be found by the litigants or their advisers.'

See *lex prospicit non respicit.*

Imperitia culpae adnumeratur 'lack of skill is counted as blameworthy'. It is *prima facie* negligent to undertake to do any act which can be done only by one with appropriate skills. One who knowingly does such an act, causing damage to another, will be negligent and liable not because he lacked the skill but because of his rash action in knowingly acting without the necessary skills. See Salmond on *Torts*, 14th edn at p. 298.

Imperium an untranslatable word of various meanings: control, empire, supreme civil authority or command of an army.

See *jus imperii.*

Imprimatur 'let it be printed'. A licence to print material; originally generally a religious or ecclesiastical book. The familiar words 'I agree and have nothing to add' spoken in the appeal courts when there are three or more judges and one or more has given judgement, are in the nature of an *imprimatur*.

Imprimis 'in the first place, principally, chiefly'.

In absentia 'in (one's) absence'. If one does not attend one's own trial one may be convicted *in absentia*. Most would object to being charged, tried and sentenced *in absentia*, but few perhaps would object to being executed *in absentia*.

In aeternum 'for eternity', for ever.
See *in perpetuum*.

In arbitrio judicis 'in the judge's discretion'. See *optima est*.

In banco 'on the bench'. Abbreviated to *in banc* this was the name given to sittings of the judges of Queen's Bench, Common Pleas and Exchequer at Westminster before these courts were abolished by the Judicature Acts 1873–5.
See *nisi prius*.

In camera 'in a chamber', in private. A judge in a courtroom or chambers sits *in camera* if the press and public are excluded. By the CPR this expression is to be superseded by 'in private'. The opposite is *in curia*.

In consimili casu 'in a like case'. A phrase of great significance in English legal history. By the 13th century the Royal Writ (written command directing action in a certain way), sealed by the Chancellor, was fundamental to the provision of civil justice. Such a document was issued with Royal authority and, in recited factual situations, provided the law and the remedy available. Despite rapid expansion of use of the new writs, the law became very rigid and in many instances wrought injustice and was wanting. The Statute of Westminster II (1285) enacted that the clerks in Chancery might agree to production of a new writ whenever there was a writ, but 'in a like case (*in consimili casu*) falling under like law and requiring like remedy is found none'. This gave rise to a crop of new forms of action known as 'actions on the case'. An accurate knowledge of the Register of

Writs and the form of action originated by each writ was basic to the professional learning of the mediaeval lawyer. If a client's case could not be fitted factually into an existing writ and likewise if it was not sufficiently close (*in consimili casu*) for the Chancery to be willing to frame a new writ, the only remedy was a petition to the King's Council: such petitions were framed in grovelling language 'humbly craving' the relief sought.

The word 'writ' continued to describe the originating process until abolished by the CPR in April 1999. Thereafter, instead of issuing a 'writ' to commence proceedings and to stop limitation running, one issued a 'Claim Form' upon which, as with the old writ, could (generally only if it could be shortly stated) be endorsed the whole claim. If it was not, the detailed claim followed the brief account of the nature of the claim, but the title of this further document 'Statement of Claim', needed to be changed to distinguish it from the originating document headed 'Claim Form' and so, following the County Court Practice, this became 'Particulars of Claim'.

In curia 'in (open) court'. The opposite is *in camera*.

In esse 'in being'. Cf. *in posse*.

In extenso 'in full *or* at full length'. Words usually abbreviated may be said to be set out *in extenso* if the full words are set out.

In extremis 'in extremity *or* at the very end', at the point of death. Used colloquially this may mean 'in a bad way'. Attributed to Voltaire (1694–1778) on his deathbed, when invited to renounce the devil, is the answer: 'This is no time to make new enemies.'

In flagrante delicto 'while the crime is ablaze'. A criminal, caught red-handed or in the act, is caught *in flagrante delicto*. Abbreviated to *in flagrante* the expression is commonly used as a discreet reference to those caught in the act of adultery or fornication. If this Latin be forbidden in the courts, the available substitutes are hideously indelicate or are not exactly synonymous: fornicating, copulating, having intercourse, shagging, making love, bonking, engaged in coition, having sex, in congress, being intimate, fucking. Since comprehension at any cost by the man in the street of court-room language seems to be the order of the day, the last mentioned word, universally understood colloquialism (but in the *Oxford English Dictionary* notwithstanding) should find favour. With its delictual connotation, however, fornicating must be the hot favourite, with the others as no more than also-rans. Such a wealth of alternative expression might suggest obsession amongst the English-speaking peoples. To abolish use of this expression in the courts would be a pity. Edward Gibbon made the point in 1796: 'My English text is chaste, and all licentious passages are left in the obscurity of a learned language.' By obscurity, he later made clear, he meant 'decent obscurity' ... good taste? These passages are often in footnotes to be decoded by those who can and want to.

Induciae legales 'days of grace'.

In forma pauperis 'in character of a pauper'. Name given to a form of appeal to the Judicial Committee of the Privy Council by which an impecunious appellant has the services of counsel and solicitors without payment of fees and is protected from any order for costs being made against him.

Infra 'below'. In literary usage denoting something that follows 'below' in a text. Often preceded by *vide*, 'see'. The opposite is *vide supra*, 'see above'.

Infra dig. Abbreviated form of *infra dignitatem* beneath (one's) dignity, undignified, inconsistent with one's position. When Lord Taylor of Gosforth was appointed Lord Chief Justice of England he was reported as saying to Lady Taylor: 'where do I go from here?' 'Into the kitchen to help with the washing up,' she replied. *Infra dig*? But when Lord Goddard was Lord Chief Justice, he told of a reluctant witness who pleaded (only after much alternate menace and cajolery) that she had received a threatening note. 'Madam,' his lordship had declared. 'I too received such a note this very morning and, sitting where I am now, ought not to tell you what I did with it sitting in another place.' *Infra dig*?

In futuro 'in the future'.

In gremio legis 'in the lap of the law'. Under the protection of the law. No man is above the law and in a civilized society we all live *in gremio legis*. *Sed quaere*, see *nulla poena* and *satius est impunitum*.

Iniquum est aliquem rei sui esse judicem 'it is unjust that anyone should be judge in his own case'. Sir Edward Coke. This was considered by the Court of Appeal in *Locabail (UK) Ltd* v *Bayfield Properties Ltd and anor*. [2000] QB 451.
    See *nemo judex in causa sua*.

In judicando esto pupillis misericors ut pater et pro viro matri illorum 'in judging be merciful to minors like a father and to their mother in place of her (dead) husband'. Inscription on a scroll held in the hand of a statue of *Sanctus Ivo* (St Yves) in the cathedral of St Tugdual at Tréguier in Brittany.
    See *Sanctus Ivo*.

Injuria sine [sometimes **absque**] **damno** 'wrong without damage'. It is a wrong against an occupier to trespass on his land, even though no damage be done. The occupier may secure an injunction to prevent repetition, even though he recovers no, or £2 nominal, damages. A person may act negligently in breach of his duty of care to another but if no damage results to that other, no actionable claim results.
    See *damnum sine injuria*.

In limine 'on the threshold'. If, to make out a claim, proof of three ingredients is required and, at the outset it appears that one cannot be proved, then the claim fails *in limine*.

In loco parentis 'in the place *or* position of a parent'. Cannot mean either 'my parents are in a train' or 'have gone mad'.

In nuce 'in a nut(shell)'. From *nux*, 'a nut'.

In pari delicto potior est conditio defendentis 'when both parties are equally villainous, the defendant's position is the stronger'. A plaintiff (claimant since CPR) may invoke the law to press his claim but, on account of his villainy, the law is less ready to assist him.

In pari materia 'in like material *or* substance', comparable, of equal relevance in an analogous case.

In perpetuum 'in perpetuity', for ever.
See *in aeternum*.

In personam 'against the person'. Rights *in personam* are rights against persons, the province of the law of obligations, in particular contract. Rights *in rem* are rights in or against a thing, realty or sometimes a chattel. A contract of mortgage gives to the mortgagee a right against the property (the thing) and may often be better than a right *in personam*, which is dependent upon the solvency of the party against whom such a right exists. In a given matter, rights *in personam* may exist against several persons and much lawyers' time and ingenuity may be taken up in practice endeavouring to find and fix one who is solvent: in particular one who is insured. Judgement is one thing; actually getting the money is quite another. Rights *in personam* are accordingly of little value as against one with no money; the proverbial 'man of straw' (the same in French, 'homme de paille').
See *in rem*.

In pleno 'in full'. Make sure he pays *in pleno*.

In posse 'in being able, in potential'. Children *in posse* are children who may come into existence. An important consideration in wills and settlements.

In private See *in camera*.

In promptu 'in readiness'.

In re 'in the matter (of)', concerning. Frequently abbreviated to *re* this is used as a heading to identify what a document is about. Thus, 're repairs at the Royal Courts of Justice'. Used also to name some reported cases: e.g., the well-known *Re Polemis* [1921] 3 KB 560.

In rem 'against the thing'. This expression has survived the linguistic cleansing of Latin from the CPR and will be found in the index to volume I of the 2005 edition and under admiralty in volume 2 at [2D-87]-[2D89] p. 358. A claim *in rem* must be in Form ADM 1. In an area of law frequently involving other nations these Latin words were in too much worldwide use to be dispensed with.
See *in personam* and *res*.

In se 'in itself *or* themselves'.

In situ 'in its place'. In its original place.

In specie 'in shape *or* form'. If I pay in gold coins and then am entitled to repayment, I may be anxious not to receive the paper money of an inflationary currency. I want repayment *in specie*, with coins of the same kind.

In statu pupillari 'in a state of pupillage'. Undergraduate or barrister's pupil.

In tenebris 'in darkness', in doubt, in the dark. In days gone by a forthright judge might have said to counsel: 'I'm afraid your argument leaves me *in tenebris*.'

Inter alia 'among other things'. A much used shorthand and doubtless a prime target for the abolitionists.

Inter alios 'among other male persons (*inter alias* 'among other feminine persons'.
See *res inter alios acta*.

Interdum stultus bene loquitur 'sometimes even a fool speaks

well'. However bad your barrister he may just have a good day.
See *rem tene*.

Interest reipublicae ut sit finis litium 'it is in the interest of the
state that there should be an end to litigation'. Basis of statutes
of limitation, of the power to strike out for want of prosecution
where delay is excessive and of the equitable doctrine of
laches.

See *finis litium, nemo debet bis, res judicata* and *vigilantibus*.

Inter nos 'between us'. Between you and me. A request for
confidentiality. *Inter nos* the judge is having an affair with the
woman solicitor in the case.

Inter pares 'among equals'.

Inter partes 'between the parties'. A court hearing is *inter partes*
where both parties attend, the one having given the other notice
of the time and place of the hearing. By the CPR this expression
is succeeded by 'with notice'. See and note *ex parte*.

Inter vivos 'between living persons'.

In terrorem 'to terrify', as a warning. A deterrent prison sentence
is *in terrorem*. Exemplary damages, to mark a defendant's outra-
geous conduct (within the narrow limits set by *Rookes* v *Barnard*
[1964] AC 1230), may be said to be awarded *in terrorem*. This
expression is colourfully mirrored by Voltaire's jibe, 'Dans ce pays-
ci (England) c'est bon de tuer de temps en temps un amiral pour
encourager les autres' ('in this country it is thought good to kill an
admiral from time to time to encourage the others'): the English
idea of a deterrent, referring to the shooting of Admiral Byng on
the quarterdeck of his own flagship for cowardice after the loss of
Minorca in 1756 following his failure to attempt relief of the garri-
son by taking on a greatly superior French force – probably the
basest scapegoat episode in British history.

Intra 'within'. Used in English as a prefix meaning within or on
the inside.

In toto 'in total, completely, entirely'. A pleading might be amended with the statement: 'The Defence is deleted *in toto*.' The pleader could then start again with a new version. But not since the CPR.

Intra vires 'within (given) powers' and therefore, usually, valid.
See *ultra vires*.

In utero 'in the womb'.

In vacuo 'in empty space'. 'It is established beyond argument that under the law of England a man is not entitled to exclusive proprietary rights in a fancy name *in vacuo*.' Mr Justice Wynn-Parry in *McCulloch* v *May Ltd* [1947] 2 All ER 708 at p. 713.

In vino veritas 'in wine the truth'. A reference to the relaxing effect of drinking wine which makes for truth by lessening inhibition and caution. Often very loosely translated as 'a drunken man tells the truth'.

Many generations of lawyers from the Temple have taken their wine in the El Vino Wine Bar at 47, Fleet Street. Founded in 1879, it is the oldest established City of London-based wine merchant and shipper. Its heyday was perhaps before the press left Fleet Street *circa* 1987. Viscount Northcliffe had his named chair.

For a barrister to have been an habitué, and to have had the fact recorded on the Lord Chancellor's secret file, used in some quarters to be thought a black mark which could weigh adversely in the latter's secret patronage allocations (see *Cancellarius*). This however did not necessarily prove fatal and need no longer be of concern since, with the abolition of the Lord Chancellor's control over patronage the appointment of judges is to pass to a Judicial Appointments Commission and a new and more transparent system for the appointing of Queen's Counsel has been set up. Very near to the Royal Courts of Justice, this place is abandoned by those who are made High Court Judges.

See *Cancellarius* and *fiat justitia*.

Ipse dixit 'he himself said it'. A statement relying for truth upon the fact that it has been said: and which is not independently justified or corroborated. A dogmatic statement.

Taken from the Greek as used by the followers of Pythagoras and quoted by Cicero in *De Natura Deorum* 1.v.10. *Ipse dixit. 'Ipse' autem erat Pythagoras* 'he himself said it'. He himself however was Pythagoras'.

> He is an Englishman!
> For he himself has said it,
> And it's greatly to his credit,
> That he is an Englishman!
> . . .
> But in spite of all temptations
> To belong to other nations,
> He remains an Englishman.
>
> HMS *Pinafore* W.S. Gilbert, 1836–1911

Note too Lord Atkin in *Liversidge* v *Anderson* [1942] AC at p. 247. 'A (government) minister given only a limited (statutory) authority cannot make for himself a valid return by merely saying "I acted as though I had authority". His *ipse dixit* avails nothing.'

See *noscitur a sociis*.

Ipsissima verba 'the very *or* exact words'.

Ipso facto 'by the fact itself', by the very fact or act.

Iras et verba locant 'they hire out their eloquence and fury'. Advocates.

J

There was no letter J in Classical Latin literature, which conventionally came to an end with Juvenal (c. AD 55–130). The letter J came to be used by Renaissance Italian Humanists to distinguish consonantal forms from non-consonantal forms of I. The expres-

*sions following are now commonly spelt with a J instead of an I
and for convenience are listed under the letter J.*

Jacta alea est 'the die is cast'. Said (according to Suetonius) by
Julius Caesar in 49 BC, when he had made the decision to lead his
army across the River Rubicon from Gaul into Italy and thus to
challenge Pompey and plunge the Roman empire into civil war.
In everyday parlance 'to cross the Rubicon' means to take a step
which involves risk and from which there can be no going back.
The expression has been used judicially in *Re Castle New Homes*
[1979] 1 WLR 1075 at p. 1089 and in *Re Pantmaenog Timber Co.
Ltd* [2001] 1 WLR 730 at p. 739.

Judicium parium suorum aut leges terrae 'the judgement of his
peers *or* the laws of the land'. By clause 39 of *Magna Carta* (see
below) '*no free man* shall be taken or imprisoned or disseised
(deprived of land) or exiled or in any way destroyed save in
accordance with this provision'. The *judicium parium* came to
be understood as trial by one's fellow citizens as opposed to
appointed state officials though for a while this was taken as
referring to social equals, and in the thirteenth century knights
were entitled to be tried only by knights. This soon disappeared.
The aristocracy, however, managed to retain an entitlement to
trial only by their fellow peers, by the House of Lords. This privilege (which could not be waived) applied to peers, their wives
and widows and to peeresses in their own right who were
charged with felony (very broadly, serious crime). It continued
until abolition by the Criminal Justice Act 1948 s. 30. The last
peer to be tried by his peers was Lord de Clifford in 1935. He
was acquitted of manslaughter.

The right to trial by jury is now regularly threatened with
restriction. In June of 2005 the Attorney-General proposed that
trial by jury be no longer available in complex fraud trials. The
Anti-Terrorism legislation had already provided for a special
secret non-jury court, namely the Special Immigration Appeals
Commission (SIAC) which hears appeals from those whom the
Home Secretary believes to be a risk to national security and
suspects of being terrorists and in consequence has made control
orders. A High Court Judge presides over the commission and has

the final say on the issue of reasonableness of belief. Specially appointed security vetted counsel may represent the appellants and, with the judge, are permitted a sight of the evidence upon which the order has been made (which evidence may have been secured by means of torture provided the Government neither procured nor connived at it). The detained persons are not permitted to see or be allowed to know this evidence so that their counsel cannot be assisted by their explanation or side of the story.

The use of evidence obtained by torture was challenged in the House of Lords. It ruled on 8th December 2005 in *A* v *Secretary of State for the Home Department* (No. 2), *The Times*, 9th December 2005. Such evidence is unacceptable in any British court. 'The use of torture corrupts and degrades the state which uses it and the legal system which accepts it' (per Lord Hoffmann). Their lordships were not unanimous on the standard of proof. The majority favoured a less strict requirement, namely that SIAC should refuse to admit, consider or heed evidence upon which the Home Secretary had relied where it could establish on the balance of probability that it had been obtained through torture.

Related to torture, a word has come to be used with new meaning – 'rendition'. It is used as bureaucratic jargon to describe the CIA's (the [US] Central Intelligence Agency's) practice of kidnapping terrorist suspects worldwide, then strong-arming them to detention centres, outside the US jurisdiction and hence not subject to the US justice system. Compare dictionary definitions of this word.

Lord Devlin's famous observation in his book *Trial by Jury* should be remembered. 'No tyrant could afford to leave a subject's freedom in the hands of twelve of his countrymen. Trial by jury is more than an instrument of justice and more than one wheel of the constitution: it is the lamp that shows that freedom lives.' Lewis Carroll (Charles Dodgson) understood the point when writing *Alice in Wonderland*: 'I'll be judge, I'll be jury, said cunning old Fury; I'll try the whole cause and condemn you to death.'

See *Magna Carta, habeas corpus, nulla poena sine lege, nulli vendemus, nullus liber homo* and *satius est impunitum.*

Jurat 'he swears'. Statement in an *affidavit* (see above) indicating where and when it was sworn followed by the signature of the person before whom it was sworn.

Jus accrescendi 'the right of increase'. The right of survivorship whereby, on the death of one joint owner of property the other becomes absolute owner of the whole. Property acquired by partners is presumed to be held by them as tenants in common. *Jus accrescendi inter mercatores locum non habet.* A *jus accrescendi* has no place among men of commerce. See *Buckley* v *Barber* [1851] 6 Exch. 164 at 179.

Jus civile 'the civil law'. The law of Rome. There developed a concept that side by side with this law peculiar to Rome, there was a more progressive element, the *jus gentium* (the law of peoples, of all nations) so called because it should be of universal application, its principles being so simple and reasonable that they must be recognized everywhere by everyone. Towards the end of the Republic, the idea of a *jus naturale* developed as a combination of both: the ideal law, conforming to reason; the sum of those principles which ought to control human conduct because they are founded in the very nature of man as a rational and social being.

Jus cogens 'compelling law'. An expression embodying a canon of international law whereby, without exception, some laws are so basic that all states are bound by them. Such laws are sometimes described as peremptory norms. They must be recognized by the whole community. A treaty or convention conflicting with such laws is to be regarded as void. There is general agreement that laws against slavery, genocide and piracy are *jus cogens*.

Jus est ars boni et aequi 'law is the art of good and the just *or* equal'. Note the observation of Lord Justice Scrutton in the case of *Gardiner* v *Heading* [1928] 2 KB 284: 'I am sure it is justice, it is probably the law for that reason.' 'Let us consider the reason of the case. For nothing is law which is not reason' per Sir John Powell in *Coggs* v *Bernard* [1703] 2, Lord Raymond, 911. *Sed quaere*. But compare Pascal: 'Justice and truth are of too fine a quality to be measured by our clumsy human instruments.'

See *accedas in curiam, justitia est constans, justitia omnibus* and *quicquid agas*.

Jus gentium 'the law of the nations *or* peoples (of the world)'.
See *jus civile*.

Jus gladii 'the law of the sword'. Rule by force or fear usually by a *de facto* military regime. Might is right.

Jus imperii 'right of the supreme administrative authority'. In I (Primo) Congreso del Partido [1983] AC 244 Lord Wilberforce effectively spoke of the Cuban Government as acting *jure imperii* 'by the right of the supreme relevant administrative authority'.
See *imperium*.

Jus naturale 'natural law'.
See *jus civile*.

Jus primae noctis 'right of the first night'. Better known as 'droit du seigneur'.

Jus quaesitum tertio 'right sought by a third party'. Other translations of this expression are to be found, namely: right sought for a third party, right on account of a third party, right acquired for a third party and right conferred upon a third party. The expression relates to the concept of privity in the law of contract. In *Dunlop* v *Selfridge* [1915] AC 847 at p. 853 Lord Haldane said: 'In the Law of England certain principles are fundamental. One is that only a person who is a party to a contract can sue upon it. Our law knows nothing of a *jus quaesitum tertio* arising by way of contract'. From time to time endeavour was made with limited success to circumvent this rule. The Contracts (Rights of Third Parties) Act 1999 however now makes provision for the enforcement of certain third party claims.

Jus sanguinis 'the right of blood'. In determining nationality one consideration is the nationality of the parents, the *jus sanguinis*.

Jus spatiandi 'right to wander at will'. It used to be thought that a right to use a path or a garden, a mere *jus spatiandi*, was incapable of becoming an easement: Re Ellenborough Park [1965] Ch. 131 established that it could become an easement.

Jus tertii 'right of a third person'. The expression is descriptive of a defence (to quantum or to a substantive claim) founded on the contention that a third party has a better right than the claimant (plaintiff). The *jus tertii* might be raised in answer to claims alleging conversion, disturbance of servitudes, nuisance etc.

In the case of conversion The Torts (Interference with Goods) Act 1977 provides that the Defendant in an action for wrongful interference shall be entitled to show, in accordance with rules of court, that a third party (the *tertius*) has a better right than the plaintiff (claimant) in respect of all or any part of the interest claimed by the plaintiff (claimant). The Act has expressly abolished any rule of law to the contrary: the *jus tertii* rule. See *Biddle* v *Bond* [1865] 6 B and S 225. Rules of court require that consideration be given to joining any alleged *tertius* as a party to the action.

Justiciarius regni 'the kingdom's administrator of justice'. The word *justiciarius* is medieval not classical Latin. The King/Queen is *justiciarius regni*. See *Darnel's* or *The Five Knights' Case* (1627) 3 St Tr 1.

Justitia est constans et perpetua voluntas jus suum cuique tribuens 'justice is the constant and perpetual wish, rendering everyone his right'. The opening words of the first title of the first book of Justinian's *Institutes de justitia et jure*, 'about justice and law'. Justinian's definition of that elusive concept justice leaves open what is the issue in every case, what is a man's due? Cf. Cicero's earlier observation: *suum cuique tribuere, ea demum summa justitia est*, 'to render to each person his due, that indeed is the ultimate justice'.

See *accedas in curiam, jus est ars boni et aequi* and *justitia omnibus*.

Justitia omnibus 'justice for all'. Note the affinity with access to justice (*accedas in curiam*) and that in the three years to 2001 the cost of commencing civil proceedings in the High Court and the County Court escalated, legal aid was greatly restricted and variation of the caution eroded the right to silence. Note too reference, in a letter from the Chairman of the Bar published by *The Times* on 2nd March, 2001, to a home secretary calling for a restriction on the right to trial by jury, for more convictions and longer sentences, for more aggressive and bullying prosecutors and for the introduction in evidence of an accused's past record.

See *accedas in curiam, jus est ars boni et aequi, justitia est constans* and *nulli vendemus*. To inquire too deeply into what is justice may be unwise: a bottomless pit opens up.

See too *accusare nemo se debet*.

L

Lacuna 'hole, chasm, defect, gap'. For a legal *lacuna* see *R* v *Duggan, The Times*, 7th November 2002 and *R* v *Horsman* [1998] QB 531.

Laesa majestas 'injured majesty'. *Crimen laesae majestatis* is a crime of high treason. In modern English lese-majesty (or lèse-majesté) is treason, an offence against the sovereign power, an insult to the sovereign, conduct which is presumptuous.

Latine dictum 'spoken in Latin'.

Latine scriptum 'written in Latin'.

Laudator temporis acti 'a praiser of times acted out . . . of times past'. Horace. The familiar observation of those who begin to grow old: 'Things aren't what they used to be.' Probably, they never were.

Legem brevem esse oportet 'a law should be brief'. Cicero. The long and convoluted Civil Jurisdiction and Judgements Act 1982 (at the time the most important chapter of community law since the European Communities Act of 1972) made clear why; and on its passage through the legislature drew the following comments:

'I rather think that it should be accompanied by a Government Health warning. There is nothing whatever I can do to make my speech short, and those who expect to find it of throbbing human interest will, I fear be wholly disappointed. The road lies uphill all the way.' Lord Hailsham, Lord Chancellor, HL, 3 December 1981, Vol. 425 col. 1126.

'This mind boggling myriad of legal complexity.' Mr Barry Porter, HC, 24 March 1982, Vol. 20, col. 1126.

'. . . this is on any showing a Bill of enormous complication. I would go further and say that the measure gives to the word complexity a new dimension.' Lord Foot, HL, 3 December 1981, Vol. 425, col. 1141.

Brevity is not the only problem with statutes. Clarity can sometimes be seriously absent. S.1 of the Road Transport Lighting Act 1967 provides:

'It is hereby declared **for the avoidance of doubt** that material designed primarily to reflect white light as light of another colour is, when reflecting light to be treated for the purposes of the principal Act as showing a light, and material capable of reflecting an image is not, when reflecting the image of a light to be so treated.'

Of course this avoids all doubt and there can be no question as to what it means! The words in bold above ought perhaps to have been followed by an exclamation mark. Note that this Act was mainly 'to resolve doubts as to the application of The Road Transport Lighting Act 1957 (the principal Act) to reflecting material'. This kind of drafting keeps lawyers in business.

Lord Denning, when considering the Land Compensation Act 1961 was moved to observe: 'I must say that rarely have I come across such a mass of obscurity, even in a statute. I cannot conceive how any ordinary person can be expected to understand it. So deep is the thicket that before the Lands Tribunal both of the very experienced counsel lost their way.'

Legem non habentis ipsi sibi sunt lex 'those having not the law are a law unto themselves'. Vulgate, *Romans* 2, v.14. Source of the familiar expression 'they are a law unto themselves' meaning that they can do as they please.

Leges fori 'laws of the forum'. Plural of *lex fori* (see below).

Legum Baccalaureus 'Bachelor of Laws', abbreviated to LLB.
See *Magister Juris* and *Legum Magister*.

Legum idcirco servi sumus ut liberi esse possimus 'we are the bondsmen of the law so that we may be free'. Cicero. Accolade for the rule of law.

Legum Magister 'Master of Laws', abbreviated to LLM.
See *Legum Baccalaureus* and *Magister Juris*.

Lex causae 'law of the cause or case'. In a matter involving conflict of laws, the *lex causae i*s the substantive law, as opposed to the law of the forum (the *lex fori*), applicable to the case. See e.g., *Harding* v *Wealands* [2006] UKHL 32 at para 30. *Leges fori* at para 48.

Lex fori 'law of the forum'. For an action to be brought in England in respect of a tort committed abroad, the common law required that conduct be actionable both by English law and by the *lex loci delicti* (see below). If these requirements were fulfilled, then in an English action for personal injury the *lex loci delicti* (i.e., the substantive law) would then still determine the rights and liabilities of the parties. From the commencement of Part III of the Private International Law (Miscellaneous Provisions) Act 1995, the provisions of this Act govern choice of law in actions of tort. Procedural matters would, however, be determined by the *lex fori* (English law). What is procedural and what is substantive may, it appears, often still be a question (see s.14 (3)(b) of the Act): this is what keeps lawyers in business. See e.g., *Harding* v *Wealands* [2006] UKHL 32 (5th July 2006). See *lex situs*.

Lex loci 'the law of the place', the law of the land. The *lex loci delicti* is the law of the country where a wrong is committed.

Lex non cogit ad impossibilia 'the law does not compel the impossible'.

Lex non cogit ad inutilia 'the law does not compel useless things'. The law will not make orders which serve no useful purpose.

Lex non scripta 'unwritten law'. the law derived from custom, tradition and usage: recognized in England by the common law, imported into it and perpetuated as the latter moves forward from precedent to precedent.

> A man may speak the thing he will;
> A land of settled government,
> A land of just and old renown,
> Where freedom broadens slowly down
> From precedent to precedent.

Alfred Lord Tennyson, through the rose-tinted spectacles of the Victorians.

Lord Denning used these words of Tennyson to introduce the Romanes Lecture 'From Precedent to Precedent' which he delivered in the Sheldonian Theatre, Oxford, on 21st May 1959.

See *accedas in curiam, nulli vendemus, ratio decidendi* and *obiter dictum*.

Lex prospicit non respicit 'the law looks forward; it does not look back'. Provisions in a statute are presumed not to have retrospective effect unless that is the clearly expressed intention of the legislature. This is one aspect of the rule of law whereby the citizen should have access to law which enables him to order lawfully his life in society. It is generally unjust to make criminal and punishable acts which did not constitute an offence at the time when they were perpetrated. Thus *nullum crimen sine lege* and *nulla poena sine lege* (see below). Determining the position may, however, be a matter of fine judgement, 'In my judgement the true principle is that Parliament is presumed not to have intended to alter the law applicable to past events and transactions in a manner which is unfair to those concerned in them, unless a contrary intention appears. It is not simply a question of classifying an enactment as retrospective or not retrospective. Rather it may be a matter of degree ... the greater the unfairness, the more it is to be expected that Parliament will make it clear if that is intended'. See Staughton LJ. *Secretary of State for Social Services* v *Tunnicliffe* [1991] 2 AER 712 at p. 724 quoted by Sir Thomas Bingham MR (as he then was) in *L'Office Clerifien* v *Yamashita Ltd* [1993] 3 WLR 266 at p. 274. See generally: Maxwell on the *Interpretation of Deeds and Statutes*, 12th edn (Sweet & Maxwell, 1997) at p. 215 and Bennion, *Statutory Interpretation*, 3rd edn (Butterworth, 1997), s. 97, p. 235.

The effect of the Human Rights Act 1998 should be borne in mind e.g. s.3 and Schedule 1, Article 7 under Part 1 of the Convention and s. (4) of schedule 2.

See *ignorantia juris neminem excusat* and *pro bono publico.*

Lex scripta 'the written law'.
See *lex non scripta.*

Lex situs 'situation law'.
The law of the place where property is situated. *Prima facie* land and immoveables are governed by the *lex situs*: a term of private international law's rule which reflects the public international law recognition of territorial sovereignty, considered by Lord Justice Rix in the Donald O'May Lecture on Maritime Law delivered 19th November 2002.
See *lex loci.*

Licet 'it is permitted'. A formal mode of granting permission. *Non licet*, 'it is not allowed'.

Lis alibi pendens 'a suit pending elsewhere'. The fact that litigation is pending between the same parties in respect of the same subject matter in another jurisdiction may enable the Defendant to secure a stay of the proceedings.
See *forum non conveniens* above.

Lis pendens 'pending suit *or* action'.

Lis sub judice 'a case *or* lawsuit before the judge'. A matter in respect of which formal proceedings have been commenced and which is being or is about to be considered by a judge and which therefore has not been decided or disposed of. If a matter is *sub judice* the media are usually precluded from reporting on it. An article in a national newspaper, published while proceedings were *sub judice* and calculated to impugn the fairness of the trial, caused collapse of the trial of the Leeds United footballers in 2001.

Litem 'suit *or* action', (accusative form of *lis*). Under the old RSC Ord. 80 r. 2 a person under disability could not bring a claim in any proceedings except by his 'next friend' and could not defend, etc., in any proceedings except by his 'guardian *ad litem*'. A person under disability was a minor/infant or a 'patient' (one with mental disorder within the meaning of the Mental Health Act 1983). Under the CPR the expression 'litigation friend' replaces both of these expressions.
See *guardian ad litem*.

Litigation friend See *litem*.

LLB See *Legum Baccalaureus*.

LLM See *Legum Magister*.

Loco citato 'in the place cited'. Abbreviated to *loc. cit.*, e.g., in a footnote, it refers to a passage previously cited.

Locum tenens 'holding the place'. Used to refer to one who stands in for a cleric or, more commonly, a doctor; a 'locum', a substitute.
See *Vicarius.*

Locus 'a place'. A position or point.

Locus classicus 'the classic place *or* source'. A reference to the most authoritative or most commonly cited passage or authority used to explain or illustrate some matter. The *locus classicus* of

Latin Grammar was (and perhaps still is) Kennedy's *Revised Latin Primer*, published by Longman.

Locus delicti 'the place of the crime'.

Locus in quo 'the place in which'. A reference to the place where something under scrutiny happened. Solicitor's instructions to counsel in accident cases used frequently to refer to the scene of the accident as the *locus in quo*.

Locus poenitentiae 'a place of repentance'. Used in the law to denote a breathing space, a time before legal obligation operates; or during which the law affords an opportunity for change of mind.

Locus sigilli 'place of the seal'. The place where a seal or notional seal used to be affixed on a deed or other document requiring it. Shown usually by a small circle containing the letters LS.

Locus standi 'place of standing', recognized position: right to appear and be heard. Only a qualified lawyer is permitted to appear in court on behalf of another. One not so qualified has no *locus standi*, though a litigant may always conduct his own case in person. One who has no right of audience (*locus standi*) may, however, assist a litigant in person by advising, prompting, taking notes, etc., so long as he does not address the court. Such a person is sometimes known as a McKenzie man (sometimes a McKenzie friend) following *McKenzie* v *McKenzie* [1971] P at p. 33. C.A.

See *Amicus curiae*.

English junior counsel may not appear in certain jurisdictions such as Hong Kong: they have no *locus standi*. English Queen's Counsel used to be able to secure *locus standi* through automatic entitlement to be called to the Hong Kong Bar. This has now been further restricted. This is not open to junior counsel and is one distortion of market forces resulting from the silk system.

See *cancellarius*.

M

Magister Juris 'Master of Law', abbreviated to M.Jur. Postgraduate law degree of Oxford University introduced in the academic year 1992–3. Like the older BCL (Bachelor of Civil Law) it is a Master's degree. The M.Jur. is a one-year taught degree for students from a non-common-law background while the BCL caters for students from a common-law background. In the year 2001–2 the M.Jur. syllabus is to include business taxation law.

Magna Carta 'the great charter'. A charter of liberty and political rights forced from King John in June 1215 on the small island of Runnymede in the River Thames near Windsor. It outlined the royal powers and rights of barons and freemen.

See *habeas corpus, judicium parium, lex prospicit, nulla poena sine lege, nullum crimen sine lege, nullus liber homo*, and *sitius est impunitum*.

Magnum opus See *opus magnum.*

Mala fide 'in bad faith'. Something done fraudulently or dishonestly is done *mala fide.*

Mala grammatica non vitiat chartam 'bad grammar does not invalidate a deed'.

Malum in se 'bad in itself', inherently bad.

Malo animo 'with bad *or* evil intent'.

Mandamus 'we command'. See *certiorari.*

Mansuetae naturae See *ferae naturae.*

Mareva This is not a Latin word but is included because it looks as if it might be and was frequently used in isolation ('A Mareva') abbreviated from 'Mareva Injunction'. Such an injunction freezes assets so as to prevent dissipation of them which might thwart a claimant's just entitlement. The name comes from a case: *Mareva Campania Naviera* v *International Bulk Carriers SA* [1975] 2 Lloyds Rep 509. Following that decision it was for the first time possible to obtain an order/injunction restraining dissipation of assets *in advance* of judgement. Initially such an injunction was granted only in the case of a foreign defendant who might remove assets from the country; but it was quickly extended. Smacking of Latin the name has been changed by the CPR and such an injunction is now called a 'freezing order'.

Mea culpa 'by my blame *or* fault', mine is the blame, I am to blame. *Mea maxima culpa*, 'mine is the greatest blame/fault', I am extremely sorry. An apology.

Me consule 'in my time as Consul'. During my stewardship or term of office.

Me judice 'I being the judge', in my judgement or opinion.

Melior est conditio possidentis 'the position of the party in possession is the better one'. Possession is nine points (parts) of the law. As against one in possession, a party who claims a better right to possession must go to the trouble and expense of invoking the law and must assess the risk and the almost inevitable, too often huge, further cost if he proves to be wrong.

See *accedas in curiam* and *esto consentiens*.

Melus improbos compescit non clementia 'it is not kindness but fear which deters the wicked'. Publilius Syrus, Maxims.

Mendacem memorem esse opportet 'a liar should have a good memory'. Quintilian, c. AD 35–100. *Institutio Oratoria* iv:ii:91. A celebrated teacher of rhetoric at Rome. Something to be remembered by those who face cross-examination.

Mens rea See *actus reus*.

Meo periculo 'at my risk'.
 See *res perit domino* and *suo periculo*.

Minor 'smaller person'. In law a person of either sex under the age of eighteen. Such a person is treated as under disability. As such he or she is subject to special procedural provisions (see e.g., *guardian ad litem, litigation friend* and *next friend*) and is bound only by certain contracts (though in the law of contract such a person used to be described as an 'Infant'). By the CPR *minor* is superseded by 'child'; unnecessarily so, since *minor* appears in the *Oxford English Dictionary*.

Minutiae 'small things, trifles'. To fuss over the *minutiae* is to waste time with unnecessary detail.

Mirabile dictu 'miraculous to say', Virgil, *Georgics* ii:30. Wonderful or amazing to relate. An expression often used with irony in relation to information or a story which is inherently unlikely, e.g., The Athenaeum 1831, 12th March 172–3. The unassuming young female relative, whom she gives in marriage to the son of her (*mirabile dictu*) honest attorney.
 See *Sanctus Ivo*.

Modus operandi 'manner of working'. The individual way a person goes about a job. The particular way in which somebody does something. An habitual criminal may be caught through the manner in which he/she has previously carried out crimes; by the *modus operandi*, e.g., a unique method of safe-breaking.

Modus vivendi 'way of living'. Lifestyle.

Moratorium A legal term (from the Latin *mora*, meaning 'delay') used to denote the legally permitted postponement of payment of a debt for a time stipulated. Sometimes it refers to the time so stipulated.

Mortis causa 'because of death'. An expression referring to contemplation of impending death as in *donatio* (giving) *mortis causa*.

Multum in parvo 'much in little'. A tabloid newspaper with all essential information concisely presented is one of which may be said *multum in parvo*.

Mutatis mutandis 'things having been changed which needed to be changed', making the necessary alterations.

Mutuum 'a loan'. A loan of personal chattels to be used up by the borrower and returned to the lender with goods of similar kind and quantity.

N

Nec clam, nec vi, nec precario 'neither secretly, nor by force, nor with permission'. A maxim relating to user of land in the law of prescription (i.e., the law's presumption that long enjoyment indicates that rights have a legal origin) as it relates to easements (e.g., rights of way, rights of light), etc.

Ne exeat regno 'lest he should go out of the kingdom'. A prerogative writ issued to restrain a person from leaving the kingdom without leave of the Crown or of the court.

Necessitas non habet leges 'necessity has no laws'.

Nemine contradicente (abbreviated to nem. con.) 'nobody speaking against', nobody dissenting, all agreed.

Nemo dat quod non habet 'nobody gives what he does not have': the basic rule relating to the passing of any ownership of land, chattels, rights, etc. There are many mainly statutorily defined exceptions, particularly in connection with the sale of goods, defining circumstances in which rights can in law be secured from a non-owner.

Nemo debet bis vexari pro una et eadem causa 'nobody

should be twice troubled or jeopardized for one and the same matter'. The basis of *res judicata* (see below) in the civil law and of *autrefois acquit* or *autrefois convict* in the criminal law. An accused is normally limited to pleading guilty or not guilty, but if he contends that he has already been acquitted or convicted on exactly the same charge or facts, he may offer whichever of these pleas is appropriate.

By S. 76 of the Criminal Justice Act 2003 substantial inroads have, however, been made into what is known as the 'double jeopardy' rule. This provides in specified circumstances for appeal by the prosecution to quash an acquittal and order a retrial of a qualifying offence, namely murder, manslaughter and other serious offences set out in Schedule 5 Part I to the Act. Application is made to the Court of Appeal if the Director of Public Prosecutions has given prior consent.

Use of Latin in the above mentioned Act is noteworthy. By S. 76(4) 'The DPP may give consent only if satisfied that ... (c) any trial pursuant to an order on the application would not be inconsistent with the obligations of the United Kingdom under Article 31 or 34 of the treaty on European Union relating to the principle of *ne bis in idem*'. These words are not explained or translated in any definition section and translate as 'lest there be twice in the same'. The (double jeopardy) practitioner had better check what articles 31 and 34 have to say!

The onus upon the prosecution should be very great. There ought to be no lessening of the incentive and obligation to get it right first time because they can have another go if necessary.

On 10th November 2005 the first application to the Court of Appeal was announced in the case of Billy Dunlop formally acquitted in 1991 after two jury disagreements when indicted for the murder of 22-year-old Julie Hogg.

See *interest reipublicae* and *res judicata*.

Nemo judex in causa sua 'nobody (should be) judge in his own case'. No judge should preside over a matter in which he has a personal interest or involvement. A canon of natural justice. A judge with an interest related to the proceedings before him should declare it and then, as appropriate, may stand down of his own accord or if asked. If this is not done, a presumption of bias arises and any decision he makes may be challenged.

In extradition proceedings related to political atrocities alleged against Chile's General Pinochet in 2000, Lord Hoffmann failed to declare his connection with Amnesty International. The House of Lords' decision had to be reheard by a differently constituted panel of Law Lords. See *Regina* v *Bow Street Metropolitan Stipendiary Magistrate ex parte Pinochet Ugarte* [2000] 1 AC 61, 119 and 147, and *Locabail (UK) Ltd* v *Bayfield Properties Ltd* [2000] QB 451 CA.

See *homines enim* and *iniquum est aliquem*.

Nescit vox missa reverti 'a word once uttered cannot be recalled'. Horace, *Ars Poetica* 390. Something for advocates to note.

Ne sutor ultra crepidam 'let the cobbler not venture beyond his sandal'. Based on the elder Pliny's *Natural History* xxxv. 85. Keep to what you know about. It becomes increasingly dangerous for lawyers to venture outside their field of expertise.

Ne Templo deesset monumentum tertii millennii incipientis hoc signum curavit erigendum Hon Soc Int Templi 'lest the Temple should be without a memorial of the start of the third millennium the Hon(ourable) Soc(iety) of the Inner Temple has caused this monument to be erected'. In Church Court between the Temple Church and the Inner Temple Hall now stands a monument erected in 2000: at the top of a column two Knights Templars mounted on a single horse reflect a practice of the knights and the history of the site. The plinth bears the above Latin inscription. The Society, one of the four Inns of Court and an august body at the heart of the law has, in face of the law's prevailing persecution of Latin usage, launched itself into the third millennium with an inscription in Latin. The plinth also bears the date AD MM. Before this inscription was set in stone, lest it reflect in erroneous Latin the message intended, there was consultation *inter alios* with a former Bishop of Ely, the head of classics at Eton and a Regius Professor at Oxford.

Nexus 'a bond *or* connection'.

Nil 'nothing'.

Nil desperandum 'nothing is to be despaired of'. Never give up. From Horace's *Odes* i:vii:27. Good advice for the advocate whose fine judgement must steer a course between irritating the judge and not being seen by the client to be feeble.
    See *homines enim*.

Nisi 'unless'. A decree *nisi* of divorce is one to be made final unless . . .

Nisi prius 'unless sooner *or* before'. Those words are sometimes to be seen painted on the wall, or cut in the oak panelling, of old courts in what were assize towns. Magna Carta and the Assize of Clarendon approved a system for the trial of serious crime on circuit. All civil actions, however, were tried in London at Westminster. Travel to London in early times was an intolerable burden. In 1285 the Statute of Westminster II provided for trial of fact in civil cases on circuit, so as to avoid fetching the parties, jurors and witnesses to Westminster. The action was, however, still started at Westminster, the preliminaries dealt with there and the sheriff ordered to have jurors there for trial on a certain day, *nisi prius* (unless before) that day the justices of assize came to the plaintiff's county. In practice it was arranged that the assize trials should be heard in the county before the date fixed for hearing by the judges sitting *in banc* (see *in banco*) at Westminster. Courts designated *nisi prius* are those which were used for this purpose.

Nocte 'by night'. Lawyers doing personal injury or professional negligence work will read doctors' and sometimes nurses' reports and notes where the word *nocte* is often found, denoting things done or drugs given or to be given in the night.

Nolite judicare, ut non judicemini 'judge not that you may not be judged'. Vulgate. St Matthew Ch 7 v. 1. Note the lesser known verse two: *in quo enim judicio judicareretis, judicabimini; et in qua mensura fueritis, remetietur vobis* . . . for what judgment you judge shall be judged; and with what measure you mete, it shall be measured to you again.

See *ab alio specta.*

Nolle prosequi 'not to wish to proceed'. The Attorney-General may at any time stop a prosecution by entering a *nolle prosequi.*

Nolo contendere 'I do not wish to contest'. A plea available in American jurisdictions with the leave of the court. Relevant in England because, on a later conviction, such a plea is not the equivalent of a conviction, even though it led to the imposition of a penalty. See Archbold, *Criminal Pleading, Evidence and Practice*, 2005 @ s 8–175.

Non compos mentis 'not (having) control of mind', of unsound mind, not in one's right mind. Opposite of *compos mentis.*

Non constat See *constat.*

Non est factum 'it is not made'. An abbreviation of: *scriptum praedictum non est factum suum*, 'the apparent writing is not (of) his making'. If a person has signed a contractual document by mistake, the document relating to a transaction of an entirely different nature from that which he thought (the category of document being different) then, provided he has not been negligent, he can plead by way of defence to any claim made against him and based on the document, that the document is not his, *non est factum.*

Non sequitur 'it does not follow'. Used as a noun to describe something which does not follow logically from what went before.

See *post hoc ergo propter hoc.*

Noscitur a sociis 'it is known from fellows *or* allies'. A rule of construction of documents and statutes. The meaning of a doubtful word may be ascertained by reference to the meaning of words associated with it.

Lawyers are eternally concerned with the exact meaning of

words but seldom does a Law Lord resort for assistance to Lewis Carroll's (Charles Dodgson's) *Through the Looking Glass*. In *Liversidge* v *Anderson* [1942] *AC the House of Lords* was concerned with the meaning of the words 'has reasonable cause to believe'. If construed objectively the courts could determine whether the Secretary of State had reasonable cause to believe. If subjectively the 'say so' (*ipse dixit*) of the Secretary of State was sufficient and he was not subject to any control by the courts. The belief in question related to whether a person was *inter alia* of hostile origin and hence one against whom a detention order could be made under the relevant wartime regulation. Their Lordships decided upon a subjective interpretation. Lord Atkin's famous dissenting speech concluded:

> I know of only one authority which might justify the suggested method of construction:
>
> 'When I use a word,' Humpty Dumpty said in rather a scornful tone, 'it means just what I choose it to mean, neither more nor less.'
>
> 'The question is,' said Alice, 'whether you can make the words mean so many different things.'
>
> 'The question is,' said Humpty Dumpty, 'which is to be master – that's all.' (*Through the Looking Glass* c. vi.)
>
> After all this long discussion the question is whether the words 'if a man has' can mean 'if a man thinks he has'. I am of the opinion that they cannot, and that the case should be decided accordingly.
>
> See *ipse dixit.*

Nota bene 'note well'. Abbreviated to NB. Observe what follows with care.

Notabilia 'notable things'.

Novissima verba 'newest *or* most recent words', last words.

Novus actus interveniens 'a new act intervening'. An expression used in the law relating to causation. If an act, subsequent to a negligent act, which latter was leading to damage, is sufficient in reality to interrupt and negative (or reduce to *de minimis* (see above)) the causative effect of the first act (to break the chain of causation) so that the second act was the real, immediate, proximate or actual cause of damage ensuing, then the perpetrator of the first act may be exonerated by *novus actus interveniens*. See generally Lord Wright in *The Oropesa* [1943] P. 32, p. 36.

Noxiae poena par esto 'let the punishment be proportionate to the guilt'. Cicero.

> My object …
> To let the punishment fit the crime …
> The billiard sharp whom anyone catches,
> His doom's extremely hard
> He's made to dwell
> In a dungeon cell …
> On a spot that's always barred.
> And there he plays extravagant matches …
> With a twisted cue
> And elliptical billiard balls.
> *The Mikado*, W.S. Gilbert 1836–1911

W.S. Gilbert was called to the Bar of the Inner Temple on 17th November 1863 and practised as a barrister for part of his life.

Nudum pactum 'a nude agreement *or* bargain'. An invalid agreement; one giving no contractual rights by reason of the absence of consideration or otherwise.

Nulla bona 'no goods *or* no property', nothing that can be distrained upon. Answer given by the sheriff when he has been authorized to seize chattels of some person in execution of a judgement and has been unable to find any goods or chattels to seize.

See *fieri facias*.

Nulla poena sine lege 'no punishment without a law'. No person can be punished except for breach of an identifiable law in force at the time of an alleged offence. There can be no arbitrary punishment at the whim of some tyrannical official. This is one aspect of the rule of law.

But note Lord Atkin in *Liversidge* v *Anderson* [1942] AC 206: 'These cases raise the issue as to the nature and limits of the authority of the Secretary of State to make orders that persons be detained under Regulation 18B of the Defence (General) Regulations 1939. The matter is of great importance both because the power to make orders is necessary for the defence of the realm and because the liberty of the subject is seriously infringed, for the order does not purport to be made for the commission of an offence against the criminal law and not by any kind of judicial officer, it is not made after any inquiry as to the facts as to which the subject is allegedly party, it cannot be reversed on any appeal and there is no limit to the period for which the detention may last.'

These words of caution should be heeded today with the dangerously authoritarian advent of the Anti-Terrorism Crime and Security Act 2001. Comparable observations alerting to such dangers were made in the House of Lords in *A and Others* v *Secretary of State for the Home Department, The Times*, 17th December 2004 and [2005] 2 WLR 87.

See *satius est impunitum*. See also *Habeas Corpus, judicium parium, lex prospicit non respicit,* Magna Carta, *nulli vendemus, nullum crimen sine lege* and *nullus liber homo*.

Nulli secundus 'second to none'.

Nulli vendemus, nulli negabimus aut differemus, rectum aut justiciam 'to nobody will we sell, to nobody will we deny or delay right or justice'. From *Magna Carta*. Sir Christopher Staughton, in the 5th Millennium Lecture to the Inner Temple, 29th November 2000, thought an amendment appropriate in the political climate of that year, namely: 'provided it doesn't cost too much'. Nothing has changed in the years to 2006. Unfortunately this was not *Latine scriptum* (see above).

See *accedas in curiam*.

Nullum crimen sine lege 'no crime without a law'. *Sed quaere* since the Anti-Terrorism Crime and Security Act 2001.

See *nulla poena sine lege*.

Nullus liber homo 'no free man'. From clause 39 of *Magna Carta*. But these words call for their own separate entry. (Refer to *judicium parium* above). They were quoted on 9th January 1770, more than once, in the speech of William Pitt, 1st Earl of Chatham, to the House of Lords as he challenged the House of Commons's right to expel John Wilkes, an elected Member whose paper, *The North Briton*, had been convicted of publishing a seditious libel.

'National rights' he said 'contained in *Magna Carta* . . . These are the rights of the great barons, or these are the rights of the great prelates; no, my Lords, they said it in the simple Latin of the times, *nullus liber homo*, and provided carefully for the meanest subject as for the greatest . . . These three words, have a meaning which interests us all; they deserve to be remembered – they are worth all the classics . . . Where law ends, there tyranny begins.'

These words and their original context in *Magna Carta* should be thought upon and heeded by the progressively authoritarian government of today.

See *habeas corpus, judicium parium, Magna Carta, nulla poena sine lege, nulli vendemus,* and *satius est impunitum.*

Nunc demum redit animus 'now at last our spirit returns'. Tacitus, Agricola, 3. Sentiment of the barrister who at last wins a case after a series of dispiriting disasters. Cf., *causam obtinere.*

Nunc pro tunc 'now for then'. An expression used to indicate that a court order is to have effect from a date earlier than that upon which it is made.

O

Obit 'he died'. Often on gravestones.

Obiter dictum 'a statement by the way', something incidental. English law follows precedent. The part of a case which is binding and must be followed is the *ratio decidendi* (the reason of deciding). If, in passing, a judge makes some observation as to the law, which is not in point, which does not relate specifically to the reasons leading directly to decision in the case before him so as not to be part of the *ratio decidendi*, that statement will be *obiter dictum* (abbreviated to *obiter*, e.g., 'what was said in that case was said *obiter*'). As such it is not binding as precedent on other judges in subsequent cases. A statement made in this way (said *obiter*) is referred to as a *dictum* (plural *dicta*). However, a *dictum* (or *dicta*) may still be of persuasive value. How great will depend upon the reputation of the judge in question. In the course of the House of Lords hearing in the case of *GE Trade Mark* [1973] RPC 297 at p. 306 a question arose as to the weight to be given to a judgement (not an *obiter dictum*) of Neville J. Lord Diplock asked counsel: 'Could you please tell me this, because I am not so familiar with the reputation of Chancery Judges: where does Neville J rank in the hierarchy between Eve J (at the top end) and Kekewich J (at the bottom end)?' Counsel replied: 'I am bound to say at the Kekewich end.' He went on: 'Neville J tried a great many cases, but apparently learnt very little!

Judicial weight (intellectual not actual) league tables are not yet available.

Odium 'general or widespread dislike'.

Omnia praesumuntur contra proferentem 'all is presumed against the (party) proferring'.

See *contra proferentem*.

Omnia praesumuntur contra spoliatorem 'all is presumed

against a wrongdoer'. Where a chattel is misappropriated by one who cannot produce and return it, the Court will assume against him the highest possible value of the item. *Armory* v *Delamirie* [1721] 1 Stra 505. See Salmond and Heuston on *Torts* [21st edition, 1996, p. 116 n. 24.] So too similarly in the case of *Infabrics Ltd* v *Jaytex Ltd* [1985] FSR 75, where solicitors, in breach of their duties to the court as officers of the court, took insufficient steps to ensure the preservation of relevant documents which bore upon the quantum of damages, this maxim was applied against them.

The expression used to be seen in pleadings.

This maxim is a resoundingly splendid example of high-minded law *Latine scriptum* (see above). Without it the law will surely be the poorer.

Some editor with a soul has, perhaps feloniously, allowed its (short term?) survival in the 2005 CPR (see note 31.10.6 at p. 762).

Omnia praesumuntur rite esse acta 'all things are presumed to have been correctly done'. A very remarkable presumption in the light of life generally.

Onus probandi 'the burden of proving'.

Op. cit. See *opere citato*.

Ope et consilio 'by aid and counsel', aid and abet.

Opere citato 'in the work cited'. Abbreviated to *op. cit.* and used as reference to a work previously cited.

Optima est lex quae minimum relinquit arbitrio judicis optimus judex qui minimum sibi 'The system of law is best which leaves least to the discretion of the judge – that judge the best who relies least on his own opinion'. Per Tindal CJ in *R* v *Darlington School* 6 QBD 682 at p. 700. See *in arbitrio*.

Opus magnum (usually *magnum opus*) 'great work'. Any writer's or artist's masterpiece.

Otiose Not a Latin word but a shorthand, much used, particularly by lawyers, meaning: serving no useful or practical purpose . . . not required or without function. The writer first noticed it as an undergraduate, whilst reading a law report in Oxford's Bodleian Library. The light pencil of another *ignoramus* had feloniously asterisked it to the margin and written 'disgusting'.

P

Pacta sunt servanda 'agreements are to be observed'. An exhortation to be found in books on public international law reflecting the fact that little more than moral imperative ensures that treaties are honoured. In a speech at the Elysée Palace on 2nd July 1965 General de Gaulle observed: *'Les traitées, voyez vous, sont comme les jeunes filles et comme les roses: ça dure ce que ça dure.'* 'Treaties you see are like young girls and roses: they last while they last.' Prime examples of the fragility of this maxim are Hitler's non-aggression pacts with Poland in 1935 and then with the Soviet Union (the Hitler–Stalin Pact) in 1939, the latter with a secret clause concerning the division of Poland! Both were cynically ignored as German troops invaded Poland and then Russia on 1st September, 1939, and on 22nd June, 1941, respectively.

An up-to-date example, scarcely less discreditable to many in its different way, was the announcement in March 2001 by the administration of George W. Bush that it had sought advice from the State Department as to how the US could legally withdraw from the Kyoto Protocol to the UN Framework Convention on Climate Change (global warming treaty) to which it had agreed at Kyoto and was a signatory but has since communicated its intention not to ratify. The protocol involved industrial nations in reducing emissions of greenhouse gases (carbon monoxide, methane and other pollutants) to 7 per cent below their 1990 level by 2012. Ratification by Russia enabled the Protocol to come into force in February of 2005 but it has been rendered of substantially less effective by the non-participation of the USA which accounts for a larger percentage of damaging world emissions than any other nation. To their great credit several American states have, in view of the central administration's abdicatory uninterest, taken it upon themselves to go it alone in taking steps to limit emissions damaging to the environment.

Pacta tertiis nec nocent nec prosunt 'treaties are not to harm or benefit third parties'. The general rule of international law is that treaties are not to confer rights, or impose liabilities, upon third parties, c.f., *res inter alios acta*.

Par in parem non habet imperium 'equals do not have authority over one another'. An expression of international law meaning that one sovereign power cannot exercise jurisdiction over another sovereign power. *Sed quaere*.

Pari passu 'at an equal step *or* equal double pace', at the same speed. Someone who works on two projects and divides his attention between them equally, works on them *pari passu*. An expression used to describe a way of distributing assets where there are competing claimants, e.g., bankruptcy.

Pari ratione 'by parity of reasoning', by equal argument.

Participes criminis 'partners in crime'. Accomplices. See *socius criminis*.

Passim 'in various places'. The word is used in text and reference books to indicate that a topic is considered here and there in the work.

Paterfamilias 'patriarch *or* head of the family'. There is not an accurate translation because there is no modern English equivalent of the relationship between the Roman father (*paterfamilias*) and his son(s). The Roman *paterfamilias* had power *vitae necisque* (of life and death) over his son, who (if he survived) in turn was liable to inherit his father's debts (a *damnosa hereditas* . . . an injurious inheritance).

Paucis verbis 'with few words'. Before Latin became forbidden in the courts, a (perhaps apocryphal) judge once said to counsel: 'After lunch please address me *paucis verbis*. On present form I fear that you may read me the Psalms.'

A formidable judge at the London Quarter Sessions in the 1960s asked an unrepresented defendant whether he wished to say anything before sentence was passed. 'F . . . off' came the reply. 'Very well, not much to say to you either: three years.' *Paucis verbis* all round. More recently, when asked whether he pleaded guilty or not guilty, an accused replied in the same vernacular. 'I translate that as not guilty' said the judge to the clerk recording the plea. Remember: *vir sapit qui pauca loquitur* 'it is a wise man who says little'.Yet *Brevis esse obscurus fio* 'when I try to be brief I become confused'. Horace, *Ars Poetica* 25.

See *contra verbosos*, *rem tene verba sequentur* and *tempus tacendi*.

Pax 'peace'. So in the days when the Roman Empire maintained an unprecedented degree of known world stability, there was the *Pax Romana*. More recently, in the heyday of the British Empire, there was the *Pax Britannica*. Now perhaps there is the *Pax Americana*: *sed quaere*. In English the same word denotes a call for peace or a truce.

Pendente lite 'while the suit is pending'.

Per 'through', usually, but it is a word of many meanings. Can mean during, according to, out of, etc. In the law it is used generally in the sense of 'according to', e.g., *per* Smith LCJ.

See *per curiam* and *per incuriam*.

Per annum 'by the year', annually or for each year. Not to be confused with *per anum*: through the rectum! There is an urban legend of a letter from the Inland Revenue referring erroneously to payment *per anum*; the recipient replied that he paid already through the nose.

Per capita 'by heads', for each person, individually.

Per curiam 'according to the court'. The expression has the meaning that a decision or statement is made by the whole court and hence is more authoritative.

See *per incuriam*.

Per diem 'by the day', daily, for each day. Medical term directing when medicine should be given or therapy applied.

Per incuriam opposite of *per curiam*. Judicial observation made without sufficient thought or even by mistake. Something not to be relied upon too heavily or at all. Sometimes means by oversight.

See *per curiam* and *obiter dictum*.

Per procurationem 'through the agency (of)'. Sometimes *per procuratorem* through his agent. Abbreviated to p.p. these expressions may be used when signing a letter or other document on behalf of another. If a secretary, Miss Smith, signs on behalf of her absent boss, Mr Jones, she should write and sign: 'Mr Jones p.p. Miss Smith' (Mr Jones through his agent Miss Smith) not 'Miss Smith p.p. Mr Jones'. Though wrong, the latter practice is not uncommon.

Per quod consortium et servitium amisit 'through which he has lost her partnership and services'. An action which used to be available to a husband against anyone who had committed a tortious act against his wife, if he could prove that thereby he was deprived for any period of her society and services. No corresponding cause of action vested in a wife. Samuel Johnson (1709–84) reflected perhaps the thinking of his times: 'Nature has given women so much power that the law has very wisely given them little.'

Per se 'through *or* in itself', intrinsically.

Per stirpes 'by *or* through branches'. An expression used technically to describe the distribution of property. Where property is left *per stirpes* to three children, the children of one (the grandchildren of the donor) will not be entitled to more than a rateable proportion of their parent's share. They will not be entitled *per capita* (see above) with the other children (their uncles and/or aunts).

Per subsequens matrimonium 'through subsequent marriage'. A child conceived out of wedlock may be made legitimate through subsequent marriage of the parents.

Persona 'person'. *Persona grata*, 'acceptable person'. *Persona non grata*, 'unacceptable person': e.g., 'he is *persona non grata* because last time he came to my house he drank too much and vomited all over my best Persian carpet'.

Placet 'it pleases'. *Non placet* .. it does not please. Used to denote agreement or disagreement. In the past, in court or ecclesiastical circles it denoted permission or assent or the opposite.

Plene administravit 'he has fully dealt with'. The defence of an administrator or executor, when sued upon the debt of a testator, that he has administered the estate and has no assets with which to satisfy the claim.

Post cibum 'after food'. Words to be found (often abbreviated to PC) in medical notes or on prescriptions, denoting that something is to be taken or administered after food.
    See *ante cibum, bis die* and *nocte*.

Post hoc; ergo propter hoc 'after this therefore on account of this'. A reference to fallacious reasoning. Because one thing follows another, it is not necessarily caused by that other thing, e.g., we all have a last meal, but it does not follow that death, following that meal, was on account of it. This self-evident information is not infrequently alluded to by coroners when dealing with the pathologist's evidence in their summings up to the jury in Coroners' Courts. Occasionally it is dignified by quotation of the Latin!
    See *non sequitur* and *propter*.

Post meridiem 'after noon *or* midday', abbreviated to p.m.

Post mortem 'after death'. A post mortem is an examination of a dead body, usually by a pathologist and with a view to determining the cause of death; an autopsy.

Post scriptum 'written afterwards', postscript, abbreviated to PS. Additional material added, often at the end of a letter.

P.P. abbreviation of *per procurationem* or *per procuratorem*.

Praecipe 'direct'. Often used as another word for a writ which directs that something be done.

Praemunire 'to fortify *or* defend'. Name given to a Statute of 1353 (reign of Edward III) directed primarily against the taking away to the Papal Curia in Rome cases which should have come into the Royal Courts. It created an offence of asserting the supremacy of the Pope over the Crown of England. Cardinal Wolsey was indicted for an offence under this Statute when he fell from favour after failing to secure an annulment of King Henry VIII's marriage to Catherine of Aragon.

Prima facie 'at first sight *or* on first impression'. A *prima facie* case is one which, subject to further scrutiny or unforeseen circumstances, seems good. Likewise with *prima facie* evidence.

Primo 'in the first place', first.

Primus inter pares 'first among equals'. 'All animals are equal but some are more equal than others.' George Orwell, *Animal Farm*, 1945.

Pro 'for *or* on behalf of'. To be *pro* means to be well disposed to. To be *pro* in an argument means to be supportive of one or other side.
  See *pro bono publico*.

Pro bono publico 'for the public good'. To do *pro bono* work is to do unpaid work for the good of the community. Legal Advice is often available on this basis through the Citizens' Advice

Bureaux. One principle governing statutory interpretation is that the construction should be for the public good and this may affect whether or not a retrospective interpretation is permissible. At the Presidential Luncheon of ILEX (The Institute of Legal Executives) in June of 2002, the then Lord Chief Justice, Lord Woolf, said: 'I think one reason why *pro bono* is not playing its part in the provision of legal services as it should, is because of the very words *pro bono*. I would like someone to provide me with a plain English substitute translation.' A competition was arranged and on 22nd November 2002 a substitute (not a translation) was announced as the winner, 'law for free'.

This new expression does not seem to have caught on. Plain but not good English and not being flexible like *pro bono*, it is of limited application. One cannot for example work 'law for free'. See *Remon* v *City of London Real Property Co Ltd* [1921] 1 KB 49 and Bennion, *Statutory Interpretation*, 3rd edn (Butterworth, 1997).

See *lex prospicit non respicit*.

Pro forma 'for form', as or being a matter of form. A *pro forma* invoice is one sent in advance of goods supplied.

Progressus per peritiam 'progress through skill (practical knowledge)'. Motto on the coat of arms of the Institute of Legal Executives (ILEX). The Latin was replaced in November 2002 by 'Progress through Knowledge'. Were skill and the practical intentionally abandoned?

Pro hac vice 'for this turn', for or on this occasion (only).

Pro patria 'for one's native country'. *Pro patria et rege*, 'for king and country' (reversed). An outmoded notion of patriotism.

Propter 'on account of'. 'How nice to see you. I'm sorry I'm just leaving. *Non propter* I assure you.' *Propter hoc*, 'on this account'. *Propter* is a word which has cropped up when lawyers argue (eternally) about causation: especially: *post hoc; ergo propter hoc* (see above).

Pro rata 'according to the rate', proportional or in proportion.

Pro tanto 'by so much', to that extent.

Pro tempore 'for the time being', abbreviated to *pro tem*.

Proximo 'in the next', abbreviation of *proximo mense*, 'in the next month'. Used in commerce.
See *ultimo*.

PS See *post scriptum*.

Q

Qua 'in the capacity of, in so far as'. 'He sends people to prison *qua* judge.' 'She was unattractive in many ways, but not *qua* woman.'

Quae fuerant vitia mores sunt 'what were vices are (now) the fashion'. Seneca.
Barristers 'corporate' entertaining and touting for work: something unthinkable, unprofessional and disciplinable not so long ago. When some barristers urged that they should be permitted use of business cards, praying in aid that these were used by accountants and solicitors, their supplications were declined; 'they are businessmen, we are gentlemen.'
It is hard to know where 'corporate' entertainment ends and bribery begins. He who greases his way travels easily. In such pursuit the noses of some are said to become brown. From *The Times* of 22 August 2001, it appears that in business the word 'bribe' is now frequently superseded by the expression 'facilitating payment', something necessary for survival in modern international commerce.
Modesty used to be a virtue and any disposition to the vulgarly commercial was unacceptable. One does not survive in the rat-race

turmoil of 2006 unless one has ample breath with which to blow one's own trumpet; and the sound offends few. But beware *malus pudor* . . . false modesty.

Quaere 'question'.
    See *sed quaere*.

Quamdiu se bene gesserint 'so long as they shall have behaved well'.
    See *durante beneplacito*.

Quantum 'how much'. Assessing the amount of damages to be paid is described in legal practice as assessing *quantum*. A case may be described as '*quantum* only' where liability is not in issue, but the amount of money payable as damages or otherwise is.

Quantum meruit 'as much as he has deserved'. A *quantum meruit* is a claim in contract or quasi-contract for reasonable remuneration in respect of services rendered.

Quantum una hora imputas? 'how much do you charge per hour?' From *Lingua Latina Occasionibus Omnibus* by Henry Beard.

Quare clausum fregit 'by which he broke the close'. The word 'close' meant enclosed land. To break into it was a trespass to land. This was an early form of trespass.
    See *vi et armis*.

Quashing order see *certiorari*.

Quasi 'as if'. So, *quasi*-contract or *quasi*-estoppel; not quite either. So too *quasi*-judicial, describing a function comparable with that of a judge e.g., the disciplinary functions of the General Medical Council and the Jockey Club. Note too *quasi*-easement; a right in the nature of an easement.
    A word, used by lawyers when they cannot define their subject matter; when perhaps they don't really know what they are talking about.

QED See *quod erat demonstrandum*.

Questio quid juris 'the question is what law (is applicable)'. A legal Latin tag used by the revolting summoner ('somnour', a minor police official of the archdeacon's court, whose job was to serve summonses *inter alia* for offences against morality): one of the company described in Geoffrey Chaucer's *Canterbury Tales*.

> And when that he well drunken had the win,
> That wold he speke no word but in Latin –
> A fewe termes had he, two or three,
> That he had lerned out of some decree;
> No wonder is . . . he heard it all the day . . .
> Ay *Questio quid juris* wold he crye.
> (General Prologue 637–41 and 646)

Quia emptores 'because purchasers'. The commencing words of a statute of 1290 and the name by which it is known. It enabled every free man to sell his lands but the purchaser held them from the vendor's lord (not the vendor). In this way subinfeudation was avoided.

Quia timet 'because he fears'. A *quia timet* injunction may be given because some wrong can be shown to threaten and is feared, even though it has not yet materialized.

Quicquid agas, prudenter agas et respice finem. Lex plus laudatur, quando ratione probatur. Thomas à Kempis, c. 1380–1471. In 1674 William Noy 'of Lincolns-Inne, late Atturney-Generall to his Sacred Majesty King Charles the First' wrote a volume entitled *The Compleat Lawyer* which was 'printed and sold by John Amery at the Peacock over against Fetter Lane in Fleetstreet'. The above Latin appears as gratuitous, unrelated general advice or information for the complete lawyer (at p. 52): 'Whatever you do, you do cautiously and reflect upon the end result . . . a law is more to be praised when it is proved (supported) by reason.'

See *Fortescue de laudibus legum Anglie* and *jus et ars*.

Quicquid plantatur solo, solo cedit 'whatever is attached to the soil cedes (becomes part of) to the soil'. A maxim relating to the law of fixtures. So, if a building is erected on land and things are permanently attached to it, the house and the objects so attached become land: they become real property (part of the realty) and are no longer chattels. They become fixtures and, as such, are so attached to the land as to become part of it. So, if a man buys a house, the fixtures come with it automatically without separate payment (e.g., fireplaces and fitted bookshelves). The deciding factor is the degree of fixation.

Qui desiderat pacem, praeparet bellum 'who desires peace, let him prepare for war'. Vegetius, 4th century AD. *Epitoma Rei Militaris*. Sometimes *si vis pacem, para bellum*. If you want peace, prepare for war. Certainly true of Britain in 1939.

Quid faciam? Invenias argentum 'what am I to do? You are to find the money'. Terence, *Phormio* 539. Often the best legal advice. To attempt delay of the inevitable is to waste money on lawyers and to incur interest charges.

See *esto consentiens*.

Quid faciat leges, ubi sola pecunia regnat 'what may laws do where only money reigns? What power has the law where only money speaks?' Petronius.

Quid leges sine moribus vanae proficiunt 'without morals what can futile laws do?' Horace.

Quid pro quo 'something for something'. Return made for a gift or favour. Thing given by way of compensation. If a large political donation is made, the *quid pro quo* may be a knighthood or even a peerage.

The idea of something for something is fundamental to the concept of consideration in the law of contract.

Qui et idoneos nos tacit ministros novi testamenti non litterae sed Spiritus littera enim occidit Spiritus autem vivicat 'who also hath made us able ministers of the new testament; not of the letter but of the spirit: *for* the letter killeth but the spirit giveth life', II *Corinthians* 3:6. Basis of the expression 'the letter of the law'. Lord Denning was the great exponent of the spirit of the law. Useful expression which may be supportive of *prima facie* unpromising legal argument.

See *est aliquid quod.*

Qui facit per alium facit per se (or **se ipsum facere videtur)** 'who does something through another does it himself (is himself seen to do it)'. Sir Edward Coke. The basis of the law of agency.

Qui non negat confitetur 'he who does not deny acknowledges'. There is no right to silence. *E curia* Staughton LJ. (from the court of Lord Justice Staughton). Note the German view: 'Keine Antwort ist auch eine Antwort' (no answer is also an answer). For a jurisprudential analysis of right to silence (an apparently relatively simple concept) see Lord Mustill in *Reg.* v *Director of Serious Fraud Office*, Ex p. Smith [1992] 3 WLR 66 p. 74 *et seq.* Note too *tempus tacendi et tempus loquendi* 'a time to keep silent and a time to speak', Vulgate, Ecclesiastes 3:7.

See *accusare se nemo debet* and *qui tacet consentit.*

Qui prior est tempore potior est jure 'he who is earlier in time is stronger in law'. A maxim of equity. Since equitable interests attach to innocents (e.g., those who are *bona fide* and/or without notice of others' interests) the interest of the one whose interest attaches first will *prima facie* prevail.

See too *aequitas sequitur legem.*

Quis custodiet ipsos custodes? 'who is to guard the guardians themselves?' Juvenal. Relevant in the case of police corruption. The European Court of Human Rights provides a good example of *quis custodiet ipsos custodes.* It is quick to condemn any threat to the independence of the judiciary in national courts. Yet its own members are appointed through a system which contains no adequate safeguards against political interference. See article by David Pannick QC, *The Times*, Law section, 21st October 2003.

Qui tacet consentit 'he who stays silent consents (is taken to consent)'. Note too *etiamsi tacent, satis dicunt* 'even though they are silent they say enough', Cicero.

See *accusare se nemo debet* and *qui non negat confitetur*.

Qui timide rogat, docet negare 'he who asks timidly courts denial'. Seneca. To be borne in mind by advocates. Not however always true. In the days of the estimable Master Jacob counsel, in difficulty accessing the assets of a fraudulent foreign business-man, sought (*ex parte*, as it then was, now 'without notice', i.e., with no representation for the other party) an unusual order supported by somewhat uncertain law. The Master read the affi-davits and began to shake his head. 'I appreciate' said counsel, sensing imminent dismissal of his application, 'that this is a tall order, but he is plainly a very bad man'. The Master smiled, 'Have tall order as asked.'

Quo animo 'with what intention'.

Quod erat demonstrandum 'which was to be shown *or* demon-strated'. An expression used as an appendage to a mathematical (particularly a geometrical) solution and meaning that the answer to the proposition to be proved is set out. Usually it is abbreviated to QED.

In early September 1995 several national newspapers carried news that use of Latin tags was to be abandoned in the Treasury because too many did not understand them. From late September 1995 the *Sunday Telegraph* ran a very successful 'learn Latin by Christmas' course. It was called 'QED' and writ-ten by Peter Jones.

In France, Francis I abandoned Latin as the language of State as long ago as 1539. An unpopular civil service jargon, *langage administratif*, grew up in its place.

A defending barrister once opened his final speech to a bucolic jury in the deepest of rural country. 'The prosecution say A, B, C . . .' he said. '. . . QED she's guilty! Well now there's a bit more to it than that. . . .'

Quod erat faciendum 'what was to be done'.

Quod vide 'see which thing'. Abbreviated to *q.v.* A reference to somewhere else in a book.

Quo jure 'by what right or law?' A questioning of authority. See *nulla poena sine lege.*

Quomodo? 'how *or* in what way?'

Quondam 'formerly, sometime'. If one's father has undergone a sex change (gender reassignment) and it is necessary therefore to introduce to another an ostensible woman as one's father, the right course might be to say: 'This is my father, *quondam vir*' (sometime man). A lawyer who once sat judicially as a recorder might, after vacating the position, describe himself as *quondam* recorder.

Quorum 'of which (persons)'. The specified number of persons who must be present to validate the proceedings of an assembly or society.

Quot homines tot sententiae 'so many men so many opinions'. A reference to how hard it is to get consensus amongst a lot of people. Terence, *Phormio* II, IV. 14 (or 1. 454). Compare: *pectoribus mores tot sunt, quot in orbe figurae,* 'there are as many characters in men as there are shapes in the world'. Ovid. A world ... comprised ... of men who are as various as the sands of the sea'. E.M. Forster. *Abinger Harvest*, 1936, notes on English characters.

Q.V. see *quod vide.*

R

Ratio decidendi 'the reason for deciding'. In English law, which follows precedent, the *ratio decidendi* (usually abbreviated and referred to as the *ratio*) in a previous case is that which must be followed. It is an extracted distillate and (broadly) incorporates a combination of facts found and law applied by the judge in that previous case which, in focus, have gone to reaching the decision. In practice, identification and extraction of a *ratio* may sometimes be difficult, particularly in an adversarial system where one party relies upon the decision in a previous case and contends for a binding *ratio* that suits his purpose. His opponent, anxious to avoid those consequences, will contend for a different *ratio*, which incorporates different facts found, and/or a different view of what law was relevant, so that that previous case can be distinguished from the matter before the court and permit escape from the consequences of being bound by it. In appellate court decisions, where two or more judgments are given, there may be different and sometimes conflicting *rationes*. Skill in clear exposition of the *ratio decidendi* in a case is one hallmark of a good lawyer.

For a case in which it is hard to discover the *ratio* see *Kleinwort Benson* v *Lincoln CC* [1998] 4 AER 513.

See *obiter dictum* and *stare decisis*.

Ratione personae, ratione materiae ratione loci 'by reason of the person, by reason of the material [substance or character], by reason of the place'.

Re 'in the matter'. On a legal document, 'in the matter of'.
See *in re*.

Reddite ergo quae sunt Caesaris, Caesari: et quae sunt Dei, Deo 'render therefore to Caesar the things that are Caesar's; and to God the things that are God's'. From the Vulgate. St Matthew Ch. 22 v. 21.

As crushing a rebuff, as any confident prosecuting counsel, cross-examining, is ever likely to receive.

The Pharisees sought to compromise Christ by tempting him to place allegiance to God before that to Caesar and asked him whether he thought it lawful to pay tribute to Caesar. Christ invited them to show him a coin of The Empire. They offered him a *denarius* (a silver Roman coin showing the head of the Emperor: Tiberius or Augustus. The latter died in

AD 14. Tiberius succeeded him and was emperor until his death in AD 37. Coins of Augustus could well have been circulating still at this indeterminate date). Christ asked them whose image and inscription was upon it. 'Caesar's' they replied triumphantly before receiving from Christ the above recorded response.

The Pharisees were silenced: verse 22 tells us *et audientes mirati sunt, et relicto eo abierunt* . . . and hearing these things they were in admiration and leaving him went their way. The coin in question is known as 'the tribute penny'.

See *Caesaris Caesari.*

Reductio ad absurdum 'reduction to absurdity'. Expression used to describe how the logical consequence(s) of a proposition leads to nonsense.

Regina 'Queen'. In England and Wales criminal prosecutions are brought by the Crown, so that the title to criminal cases reported, or proceedings once a prosecution has been commenced is, e.g., *Regina* v (*versus*) *Smith*. In practice, when speaking, the word *versus* is seldom used: 'and' is substituted. Thus *Regina* v *Smith* is described as: 'The Queen *and* Smith'. Equally in a civil case *Smith* v (*versus*) *Jones* is spoken of as 'Smith *and* Jones'. When in October 2002 the Princess Royal was prosecuted under The Dangerous Dogs Act 1991 (for being in possession of a dog that was dangerously out of control) the case was listed as '*Regina* v *Laurence, Anne Elizabeth Alice*'. Technically she was prosecuted by her mother. But there could not be a case of *Regina* v *Regina*.

In the United States a criminal prosecution is described for example as 'The People *versus* Jones'.

See *contra pacem, fons justitiae* and *justiciarius regni.*

Rem tene verba sequentur 'keep to the point and the words will come (follow)'. Good advice for the tongue-tied advocate for which that great orator Marcus Porcius Cato (234–149 BC) is for ever to be remembered.

See *interdum stultus.*

Res 'a thing'. Note *in rem* and *in personam*. At page 359 of volume 2 of the 2005 CPR @ 2D-89 under Admiralty appears the information 'a wartime compensation was held not to be a *res* or represent a *res*'. The Eva 1950 84 Ll.L. R 20. A *res* is an object against which a claim *in rem* can properly be directed. *Res* is the nominative and *rem* the accusative case of the word *res* which means 'a thing'.

Res extincta 'a thing extinguished *or* no longer existing'. If, unknown to parties, the specific subject matter of a contract is non-existent, then (*prima facie*) no contract ensues.

Res gestae 'things done, exploits', in the sense of circumstantial matters. An expression used in the law relating to admissibility of evidence. A fact may be relevant to a matter in issue because it throws light on it by reason of time, place or circumstance, because it is part of the *res gestae*, an unmeaning term which according to Sir Frederick Pollock 'merely fudges the truth that there is no universal formula for all kinds of relevancy'. It is an imprecise concept associated in particular with a number of exceptions to the rule against hearsay; spoken of by Professor Julius Stone at 55 LQR 660 as 'the lurking place of a motley crowd of conceptions in mutual conflict and reciprocating chaos'.

Lord Blackburn's contribution was perhaps of the greatest practical value to the practising lawyer: 'If you want to tender inadmissible evidence, say it is part of the *res gestae*.' Cross, *Evidence* (Butterworth, 1958), footnote at p. 30.

For those who remember the television courtroom drama series, 'Perry Mason', endless evidence was astonishingly admitted as part of the *res gestae*. These words appear still in the 2005 edition of Archbold, *Criminal Evidence, Pleading and Practice* @ 4:291 'evidence at trial *res gestae* statements' (and in the index @ p. 2882).

Res integra 'a matter untouched', i.e., undecided. An expression used, particularly in the law, where a matter is not covered by earlier authority, so that, to reach a decision it is necessary to work from general principles. If there is a point on which there is no authority, it is sometimes described as *res integra*, e.g., a judge might say: 'This matter appears to be *res integra*, so I shall have to work from first principles.'

Res inter alios acta alteri nocere non debet 'a matter concluded between other persons ought not to hurt (disadvantage) another'. A person ought not to be prejudiced by matters transacted between another. The first four words of this expression were used judicially, by Lord Hoffmann in *Dimond* v *Lovell* [2000] 2 WLR 1121 p. 1131–2. See Preface. Cf., *pacta tertiis*.

Res ipsa loquitur 'the thing speaks for itself' (literally 'the thing itself speaks'). Probably the layman's favourite legal Latin maxim, this is the label for an area of law concerned with the incidence of burden of proof. In the law of tort ordinarily it is for a plaintiff (claimant) to prove negligence against a defendant from whom he claims damages. However, if a proven fact shouts negligence (itself speaks) against one who had control over what happened in circumstances where the claimant can have no idea of how the accident came about, then it will be for the defendant to give an explanation which is consistent with no fault on his part (if he can). For example, if a barrel rolls out of a warehouse and on to a passer-by and injures him, then, *prima facie*, the injured claimant need do no more than prove these facts, leaving the onus upon those in occupation and control of the warehouse to show how and why this was not their fault, if they can. The concept is relatively simply stated but the law is not without complication or always easy to apply in practice.

This expression (in Latin) has been attacked judicially (see Preface) and may disappear from the law. It is, however, still firmly entrenched in legal text books and is retained as a useful label in Bullen and Leake and Jacob's *Precedents of Pleadings*, 15th edn (Sweet and Maxwell, 2004), vol. 2, 71–S7, p. 1108, though it is not now included in specimen pleadings.

After recital of the facts in a pleading it was not uncommon to see the succinct statement: 'the Plaintiff will rely upon *res ipsa loquitur*.' More verbiage in English is now necessary, e.g.: 'The claimant contends in the premises that no inference can be drawn other than that the Defendant was negligent.'

The expression is based on Cicero. *Res loquitur ipsa, quae semper valeat plurimum.* The fact itself speaks and that is always of the utmost value. *Pro Milone* 53.

With this maxim goes an old story related to a number of well-known legal figures: in particular to a nineteenth/twentieth century Irishman, Serjeant Sullivan. 'Mr Sullivan,' said the judge, 'this would appear to be a case of *res ipsa loquitur*. Is that an expression with which you are familiar?' 'Why my Lord, I am indeed, very familiar: in the vales of southern Ireland, whence I hail, the people talk of little else.'

Res judicata 'a matter which has been adjudicated upon'. If a claimant seeks to litigate a claim all over again, then a defendant may answer it with the plea *res judicata*, 'exactly the same matter has been decided already'. The doctrine of *res judicata* rests upon twin principles which cannot be better expressed than in the terms of the two Latin maxims *interest reipublicae ut sit finis litium* (see above) and *nemo debet bis vexari pro una et eadem causa* (see above). See *Thrasyvoulou* v *S. of S. for the Environment* [1990] 2 AC 273 per Lord Bridge of Harwich at p. 289.

Doctrine considered by Lightman J on 7th November 2002 in *R (Opoku)* v *Principal and Governors of Southwark College.*

Res nullius 'something belonging to nobody'.
See too *bona vacantia.*

Res perit domino 'the thing perishes to or for the owner', i.e., it is at the owner's risk. Cf., *suo periculo* and *meo periculo* 'at his risk' and 'at my risk' respectively. If, while the sale of a Ming vase is being negotiated, it falls to the ground and smashes to smithereens it may be a question as to how far the law adjudges the transaction to have advanced and therefore who bore the risk at that moment. Might the purchaser have just bought, become owner of and have to pay for the smithereens? On 12th July 2005 a rare ceramic 14th century Chinese vase was sold at auction at Christie's for £15.68 million. Don't drop it!

Respondeat superior 'let the superior answer'. A superior may be responsible for what he requires a subordinate to do. Some accused war criminals have pleaded *respondeat superior* on the basis that they did no more than, as a matter of duty (being a mere cog in the military wheel), they were required to do, so that they are exonerated, all responsibility resting with their superior(s).

Res publica 'public matter', state, republic, empire.

Res sua 'thing of his own'. If A agrees to buy from B something (*res sua*) which both parties believe belong to B, but which in fact belongs to A, there will be no contract.

Res vendita 'thing sold'. See *caveat emptor.*

Restitutio in integrum 'restoration to the unchanged'. Restoration to a pre-existing position. Following misrepresentation one remedy open to the misrepresentee may be to rescind (set aside) the contract but only if he is willing and able to make *restitutio in integrum*: e.g., a misrepresentee cannot recover the price of and keep goods. To recover the price he must be in a position to and intend to give back the goods.

Rex 'King'. See note to *regina*, substituting *rex mutatis mutandis.*

Rex non potest peccare 'the King can do no wrong'.
    See *fons justitiae.*

Rex nunquam moritur 'the King never dies'. Words expressing the theory of a continuing monarchy. 'The King is dead. Long live the King.'

Rigor mortis 'the stiffness of death'. The stiffening of the body after death. Use of this familiar expression will presumably not be banned in the courts: particularly the Coroners' Courts.

Ruat caelum 'though the heavens fall', come what may.
See *fiat justitia*.

Rubicon see *jacta alea est*.

S

Salus populi suprema lex esto 'let the welfare of the people be
the paramount law'. Cicero, *De Legibus* III viii 8. Also *suprema
est lex*; 'there is not anything in the world so much abused as that
sentence.' John Selden, 1584–1654, an eminent lawyer, writer and
bencher of the Inner Temple. He lies buried in the Temple
Church in London, where his tombstone can be seen at a lower
level through glass set in the floor.

**Sanctus Ivo erat Brito. Advocatus et non latro. Res miranda
populo.** 'St Ivo was a Breton. A lawyer and not a robber.
Something miraculous to the people.' He is thought to be the
man depicted in a well-known painting of about 1450 from the
workshop of Rogier van der Weyden, which is in London's
National Gallery. The above inscription was on the information panel of this painting 'Man Reading (St Ivo)' when the
work was first displayed at the Gallery shortly after its acqui-
sition in 1971. The curator, Martin Davies, translated the Latin
loosely but tellingly thus: 'Saint Ivo was of Brittany; a lawyer
and, wonder of wonders, was not a robber.' Lawyers are used
to this. Mark Twain thought: 'The mere title of lawyer is
enough to deprive a man of public confidence.' Shakespeare
wrote: 'The first thing we do, let's kill all the lawyers' (*Henry
VI*, Part 2) and Christ said: 'Woe unto you also ye lawyers! for
ye lade men with burdens grievous to be borne, and ye yourselves touch not the burdens with one of your fingers' (Luke
11:46).
St Ivo (St Yves Hélory, 1253–1303), patron saint of lawyers,

hailed from Tréguier in Brittany and was an amazingly different lawyer: 'Whoever suffers injustice turns to him.' His statue, holding a scroll (see *in judicando esto*), is to be found in the fourteenth to fifteenth-century cathedral of St Tugdual at Tréguier, where each year on the third Sunday in May lawyers can restore (redeem?) themselves during the 'Pardon de Saint Yves'. See *mirabile dictu*.

Satius est impunitum relinqui facinus nocentia quam innocentem damnari 'it is better that the misdeeds of the guilty man go unpunished than that an innocent man be condemned.' Ulpian.

Ulpian and Papinian (and Gaius, see above) were three of the great names among Roman jurists whose work was drawn upon by Justinian (see above). But it was sometimes dangerous to pronounce upon the law. Ulpian was assassinated by the Praetorian guard in 228 and Papinian was put to death in 212 for refusing to justify the Emperor Caracalla's murder of his brother Geta. Many who have done jury service may, in connection with the burden and standard of proof, have heard it said: 'Better that the guilty go free than that the innocent be punished'. The British are not used to arbitrary arrest and detention without charge or trial. They refer vaguely but confidently to Magna Carta as the custodian of their liberty. No longer would that enactment always help them and invoke the protection of the courts by an investigation of the legality of their detention.

Since the terrorist attack in America on 11th September 2001 the British Government has sought to protect its citizens from imminent terrorist threat by measures purporting to maintain security and uphold democracy. It is beyond the scope of this book to describe and analyse the provisions and effect of the (prior) Terrorism Act 2000, the Anti-Terrorism, Crime and Security Act 2001 and the Prevention of Terrorism Act 2005. Suffice it to say that they contain disturbing curbs on the liberty of the citizen and shift in some areas the entitlement and power to detain from the judiciary to the executive: and on the basis of questionable evidence coming often from abroad and obtained possibly by torture. Notwithstanding there was still an appalling terrorist attack in London in July 2005.

Building on the above identified legislation, the Government introduced in November 2005 a Terrorism Bill. *Inter alia* this proposed offences relating to terrorism (glorifying, exalting or celebrating any terrorist act, encouraging terrorism, offering terrorist training, acts preparatory to terrorism, etc.: offences of questionable necessity, often hard to define, arguably counter-productive and endangering on occasion reasonable freedom of speech. See article of David Pannick QC, *The Times* law section 22nd November 2005). It sought to extend from 14 to 90 days the period for which terror suspects arrested by police might be held without charge. The House of Commons settled for 28 days with access to a High Court Judge for review every 7 days and the provision to be reviewed after a year. But was any increase on 14 days really necessary?

On 9th November 2005, the Prime Minister, Tony Blair, reacted in the House of Commons with apparent surprise. 'Did the right honourable gentleman say police state?' he said. Note that on 4th February 1933 Hermann Goering as president of the German Reichstag introduced a 90-day detention without charge or trial law as part of a Decree for the Protection of the German People.

See *habeas corpus, judicium parium, Magna Carta, nulla poena sine lege, nulli vendemus, nullus liber homo.*

Scienter 'knowingly'. This word was used in the context of legal liability for damage done by animals. In the case of an animal not ordinarily dangerous but which *contra naturam*, 'contrary to its nature', had behaved dangerously and caused injury or damage, broadly it was necessary for a plaintiff (claimant) to show *scienter*, namely that this propensity was known to the owner or keeper. The Latin word is not now used.

See *ferae naturae* and *mansuetae naturae.*

Scilicet 'one is permitted to know', namely, that is to say. Abbreviated to *sc.* An introduction of explanation.

Scintilla 'spark', smallest part of a thing. It will often be heard said in the courts; 'There is not one *scintilla* of evidence to suggest . . .'

See *excelsior.*

Scire facias 'you are to make known'. Name of a writ.

Sed quaere 'but question'. Used to pose a query following statement of a proposition. So in *Snook* v *Mannion* [1982] Crim LR 601, a case which turned upon entitlement of police officers to remain on premises, it was held that the words 'fuck off' used by the accused occupier were vulgar abuse and insufficient to revoke their licence to be there. *Sed quaere*, if these words were not clear enough, what expression might be? Powerful legal intellects in higher courts may yet have to ponder again these words and decide finally.

Semble Not Latin, but Law-French. Often encountered, however, it means 'it seems (that)'; usually when the authority for a proposition is weak, unclear or otherwise unsatisfactory. Frequently it refers to a statement which is *obiter* (see above).

Sensu stricto 'in the strict sense' (literally in the compressed or tightened sense). Often rendered as *stricto sensu*. In the narrow sense of an expression. *Lato sensu* 'in the broad sense' is the opposite but is seldom used.

Seq. Short for *sequens, sequentia*, singular and plural respectively, 'following'. For example *et seq.* 'and the following'.

Seriatim 'in series *or* one after the other'. A word used in pleading, especially in defences as an omnibus 'belt and braces' denial (since any allegation not specifically pleaded to will be taken to be admitted). For example: 'Save as is hereinbefore specifically admitted, denied or otherwise pleaded to, each and every allegation set out and averred by the Statement of Claim is denied as though each were set out and traversed *seriatim*.' This would now be struck out as being insufficiently clear English and unlikely to be understood by the man in the street. *Seriatim* is a useful shorthand word which will undoubtedly be missed.

Shyster Not Latin: of uncertain origin. An essential entry in a flexible work directed primarily to lawyers. The word is not mere vulgar abuse as is often thought. It is a noun, used colloquially, especially of lawyers, referring to one who achieves his ends by means which are unscrupulous.

Sic 'thus'. Used following a word, which has the first-sight appearance of being a misprint, a misspelling or otherwise in error, to indicate that what is written is what was intended by the writer or was written without qualification by an original author who is quoted: to indicate that what the document shows is right, confirming that what is written is indeed correct.

Sic utere tuo ut alienum non laedas 'use your own in such a way that you do not injure (hurt) another'. An obligation of landowners and a fundamental of the law of nuisance.

Sigillum 'seal'.
See *locus sigilli*.

Similiter 'similarly'.

Simpliciter 'simply *or* without qualification'. Negligence *simpliciter* does not equal the tort of negligence: to amount to that tort and make damages recoverable in respect of injury or loss, a negligent act must amount to a breach of the legal duty of care and must also be a cause of resulting injury or loss (damage).
See *injuria sine damnum*.

Sine die 'without a day', until a date unspecified, with no appointed date, indefinitely. If a trial is adjourned, and no date is fixed for resumption, it is adjourned *sine die*. This expression looks ripe for abolition but it does appear in leading dictionaries of the English language.

Sine dubio 'without doubt'.

Sine ira et studio 'without ill-will and without favour'. The judicial oath in England is: 'to do right to all manner of people after the laws and usages of this realm, without fear or favour, affection or illwill (*sic*)'. See Supreme Court of Judicature (Consolidation) Act 1925 and the Promissory Oaths Act 1868.

Sine mora 'without delay'.

Sine qua non 'without which not', the ultimate fundamental, an indispensable condition. Oxygen is a without which not of human life.
See *causa sine qua non*.

Sinistra manu 'with the left hand'.
See *dextra manu*.

Socius 'an ally *or* comrade'. A fellow, partner, associate.

Socius criminis 'an ally in crime', partner in crime.
See *participles criminis*.

Solatium 'consolation'. Under the Fatal Accident Acts, beginning with that of 1846, nothing could be claimed in respect of *solatium* for mental suffering and bereavement in respect of a person's death by dependants given a cause of action under the Acts. Damages were to be a matter of hard cash, reflecting and measured by the loss of pecuniary advantage to the plantiff (claimant) consequent upon the death. The Administration of Justice Act, amending the Fatal Accidents Act 1976, remedied this in 1982 and permitted damages for bereavement to be recovered in the cases, broadly, of spouses and children. A sum of £3,500 was fixed and was subject to variation by statutory instrument directed by order of the Lord Chancellor. The sum was raised in 1991 to £7,500 and again to £10,000 for causes of action accruing after 1st April 2002. A measure of inflation.
Solatium in Scottish law is the equivalent of general damages for pain, suffering and loss of amenity in the English law of tort.

Solus 'alone.' Feminine form *sola*.

Solventur risu tabulae: tu missus abibis 'the bills (the case) will be dismissed amidst laughter: you will be sent away'. Horace, *Satires*, II. i.86. You will be laughed out of court.

Solvuntur tabulae 'accounts are settled', the bills are dismissed. The defendant is absolved.

Spero meliora 'I hope for better things'. Thought of the disappointed barrister as his mind turns to the appeal court.

Sponsor 'one who pledges surety'; one who stands behind another's obligation; as one who affords a guarantee or an indemnity. To go bail is to stand surety. To *sponsor* test-match cricket or those raising money for charity does not have the same meaning: such a person is a promoter or supporter.

Sponte sua 'by his own choice', of one's own accord. Usually rendered as *sua sponte*.

Stare decisis 'to stand by decided matters'. The doctrine of precedent: note *obiter dictum* and *ratio decidendi*.

Status 'condition, state *or* status'.
　　See *status quo*.

Status quo 'the state in which'. The existing state of affairs. The *status quo ante* is the state of affairs existing before some event.

Stet 'let it stand'. When a correction or alteration has been made in writing, and cancellation of the correction or alteration is desired, so that what went before stands, this may be directed in useful shorthand by the word *stet*.

Stricto sensu see *sensu stricto*.

Sua sponte see *sponte sua*.

Suaviter in modo fortiter in re see *fortiter in re suaviter in modo*.

Sub judice see *lis sub judice*.

Sub nomine Abbreviated to *sub nom*, 'under a specified name', e.g., 'see below *sub nom*, Smith'.

Subpoena 'under penalty'. The name of a writ requiring that a person to whom it is directed should appear at a time and place specified and for a purpose stated, under penalty. Such a writ is directed to witnesses to ensure their attendance at court. Non-compliance is a contempt of court punishable with fine or imprisonment. The party causing the issue of a *subpoena* must pay the reasonable expenses of the person to whom it is directed.

There are two types: (1) *subpoena ad testificandum:* a summons to attend and give evidence *viva voce* (see below); (2) *subpoena duces tecum:* a summons to attend and bring specified documents. *Duces tecum* means 'you will bring with you'. *Subpoenas* are not used in the criminal courts. Witness orders are issued under s. 8 of the Criminal Procedure (Attendance of Witnesses) Act 1965.

Sub rosa 'under the rose'. The rose appears to have been a Roman symbol of secrecy. The expression is used to mean that something is secret or in confidence. Where a mole in the civil service leaks a government document (officially or unofficially) to the media, the transaction is *sub rosa*. Until the budget speech the Chancellor of the Exchequer's new measures are supposed to be kept *sub rosa*.

Suggestio falsi 'suggestion of untrue things'.
See *suppressio veri*.

Sui generis 'of its own kind', unique.

Sui juris 'in his own right'. Adult: recognized by the law as responsible; not a *minor* (see above) infant or child. Not a 'patient', i.e., one of unsound mind.

Summa itaque ope et alacri studio has leges nostras accipite vosmet ipsos sic eruditos ostendite ut spes vos pulcherrima foveat, toto legitimo opere perfecto, posse etiam nostram rem publicam in partibus ejus vobis credentia gubernare 'receive therefore with eagerness, and study with cheerful diligence, these our laws, and show yourselves persons of such learning that you may conceive the flattering hope of yourselves being able, when your courses of legal study are completed, to govern our empire in the different parts that may be entrusted to your care'. Extract from the preface to the Institutes of Justinian. The emperor certainly envisaged remarkably diligent, enthusiastic and ambitious law students.

See *Justitia est*.

Summa jus saepe summa injuria 'the strictest law often makes for the greatest injustice'. Cicero De Officiis 1, 33.

Summum bonum 'The highest or peak of good' i.e., the supreme or chief good. Often used to exaggerate jokingly. There are those who might say that restoration of a user-friendly attitude towards use of Latin in the law would be *summum bonum*. There is precedent for the restoration of Latin to the language of the law. See preface at p. 15.

Sum quod eris; fui quod es 'I am what you will be. I was what you are'. Epitaph on a gravestone, or thought of a generous judge about an able advocate?

Suo periculo 'at his risk'.

Suppressio veri 'suppression of the truth'. The same thing may at once be a *suppressio veri* and a *suggestio falsi*.

See *suggestio falsi*.

Supra 'above'. Used in books. *Vide supra*, 'see above'.

Suspendatur per collum 'let him be hanged by the neck'. The death penalty in peacetime was done away with on 27th January, 1999 when the UK government signed up to the sixth protocol of the European Convention on Human Rights. Not so very long ago 'Cross and Jones', *Introduction to Criminal Law* (Butterworth and Co. 1953 edition), recorded: 'Sentence of death is limited to four crimes: treason, murder, piracy with violence and setting fire to Her Majesty's ships.... Such a sentence is now carried out by hanging, although there are certain obsolete powers still in existence which enable it to be carried out otherwise.'

Some doggerel rhyming Latin used to be written in children's books:

Hic liber est meus.
Testis est Deus.
Si quis furetur
Per collum pendetur.
'This book is mine, God is witness. Should anyone steal it, he is to be hanged by the neck'.

T

Tabula in (ex) naufragio 'plank in (out of) a shipwreck'. Rescue. Means of survival. Thing that saves the day. Often used metaphorically: e.g., trial adjourned or opponent sick when advocate has had insufficient time for proper preparation? In his *Digest of Criminal Law* (9th edition, p.10 n.2) Sir James Stephen considered the criminal liability of one involved in some hypothetical factual situations not covered by the famous case of *R* v *Dudley and Stephens* [1884], 14 Q.B.D. 273 (in which shipwrecked sailors killed and ate the cabin boy) including that of two shipwrecked mariners who clung to a plank sufficient to keep only one afloat: one survived by pushing the other off.

Tabula rasa 'a scraped tablet', i.e., one from which the writing has been removed, a clean sheet or slate. An expression used often of a mind uninfluenced by preconception.

A perhaps apocryphal exchange between counsel and a judge goes thus:

Counsel: 'Is your Lordship familiar with the somewhat esoteric subject matter of this case?'

Judge: 'I think I can say that I am *tabula rasa*.'

Counsel: 'My Latin is regrettably rusty and was never good. Does your Lordship say that he has an open or a vacant mind?'

Talis qualis 'such like, such as', such as it is.

Tantum quantum 'just as much as'.

Tempus tacendi et tempus loquendi 'time to keep silent and a time to speak'. Vulgate, Ecclesiastes 3:7. A piece of the scriptures for advocates to think hard upon. Often read in its fuller context at funerals.

    See *paucis verbis*.

Terminus a quo 'end point from which', starting point.

Terminus ad quem 'end point to which', finishing point.

Terra nullius 'nobody's land'. Land subject to nobody's ownership.

Tertius 'third'.

    See *Jus tertii*.

Testator 'testator', one who has made a will or who dies testate (i.e., having made a will).

Testis unus, testis nullius 'one witness (is) a witness of nothing'. Take care with the testimony of only one witness or with only one source of evidence.

Totidem verbis 'in so many words'.

Toties quoties 'the one as often as the other'.

U

Uberrimae fidei 'of the most abundant *or* utmost (good) faith'. With some contracts one party is in possession of all the material facts and the law requires that he make full and honest disclosure to the other party. If this is not done, the contract is voidable, may be set aside. These are called contracts *uberrimae fidei*. The most common are contracts of insurance. Far too many people are unaware of the very great dangers which lie in not making full and frank disclosure to their insurers. They should respond truthfully and accurately to questions asked at the inception of the insurance and should note and respond likewise to the questions on renewal notices, which too few even notice.

Ubi jus ibi remedium 'where there is law (a right) there is a remedy'. If the law provides a right it follows that it provides a remedy for violation of it. Note Lord Rodger of Earlsferry's use of a varied and reverse form in *Harding* v *Wealands* [2006] UKHL 32. 'In that context, the brocard (elementary principle) *ubi remedium ibi jus* would be an unsafe guiding principle.'

Ulterior 'more distant, further away'. Ulterior motive: one which is concealed, not obvious or not admitted.

Ultima ratio 'the final reason'. *Ultima ratio regum* 'the last argument of kings'. Inscription on a cannon.

Ultimo Abbreviation of *ultimo mense*, 'last month'. Reference in a letter (especially in commerce) to 28th *ultimo* means the 28th of last month.
See *proximo*.

Ultra vires 'over *or* outside powers', beyond or in excess of authority or given powers. A judge acts *ultra vires* if he sentences someone to death, since the law affords him no power to do so.

Regulations made under statutory powers specifically to regulate the production of pesticides would be *ultra vires* in so far as they purported also to regulate the production of cigarettes. As a general rule a provision, act or decision which is *ultra vires* is void and of no effect.

Una voce 'with one voice', unanimously.

Uno animo 'with one mind *or* intent'.

V

Vade-mecum 'go with me'. The expression is used in English as a noun referring generally to a book containing information, to which there is or may be the need for regular reference, and which is small, light and manageable enough to be carried about in a bag or a pocket. A constant companion or manual.

Vale 'goodbye'.

Venire de novo 'to come anew', make a fresh start. The name of a writ issued by the Queen's Bench vacating the verdict of a lower court and directing the sheriff to summon fresh jurors. See *Regina* v *Rose* [1982] AC 822.

Verba chartarum fortius accipiuntur contra proferentem 'words in a document are taken more strongly against the party proferring the document'. A rule of construction and interpretation of documents and statutes.
   See *contra proferentem*.

Verbatim 'word for word', in the same words exactly. One supposes that continued use of this word may be permitted in the courts. Featuring in dictionaries of the English language it stands a better chance than *seriatim* (which in fact appears in *Chambers Twentieth Century Dictionary*).

Veritas 'truth'. Christ said: 'Everyone that is of truth heareth my voice. Pilate said unto him, what is truth?' St John 18:38. Christ's answer, if any, is not recorded. A witness swears to tell the truth the whole truth and nothing but the truth. He is not dealing with ultimate truths. He undertakes (expert witnesses apart) to testify as to what, to the best of his first-hand recollection, knowledge and belief, is fact.

The notorious Judge Jeffreys at the bloody assizes of 1685 (following the crushing defeat at Sedgemoor of the protestant Duke of Monmouth who had sought to oust the Catholic King James II) was ruthlessly indifferent to the truth of any evidence which did not go to guilt. A passage from the trial of Lady Alice Lisle (a frail widow of over seventy, who had taken pity on a wretched fugitive) illustrates behaviour that would outrage today. Judge to witness: 'Mr Dunne, have a care for it may be that more of this is known than you think.'

'My lord I tell the truth.'

'Well I only bid you have a care. Truth never wants subterfuge, it always likes to appear naked, it needs no enamelling nor any covering. But lying, canting and snivelling always appear in masquerade . . . you are a prevaricating, lying, snivelling rascal.'

In 2006 there are those parents who worry that they disadvantage their children by advocating honesty and truth. But we are still relatively a free society and ' . . . who ever knew truth put to the worse in a free and open encounter', John Milton, *Areopagitica* (1644).

Versus 'towards *or* against'. So case names. *Regina* v (*versus*) *Smith* or *Rylands* v (*versus*) *Fletcher*.

See *regina*.

Via 'by way, road, path or street'. Used in English as a preposition, 'by way of' or 'through'. One may travel on Eurostar to Paris from London, Waterloo to Gare du Nord (and back) *via* Ashford International in Kent.

Vicarius 'substitute or deputy'. So there is in law the derivative 'vicarious' liability. The law imposes upon an employer a substituted or vicarious liability for the torts of his employees committed in the course of their employment. This liability is in addition to that of the employee, who is not relieved of his primary liability.

Vice versa 'the position being reversed', conversely, the other way round.

Vide 'see', consult. Used as an instruction in a reference to a passage in a book.

Videlicet 'it is permitted to see', namely. Usually expressed by the word *viz.*

Vi et armis 'by force and arms'. One early form of trespass.
See *quare clausum fregit*.

Vigilantibus non dormientibus serviunt leges (*or* subveniunt leges, subveniunt jura, succurrit lex) 'laws serve (come to the assistance of or, the law assists) those who are vigilant not those who sleep' (note Latin's economy of words compared with the English). A maxim of equity which refused stale demands from those who had acquiesced and slept on their rights. Equity aids the vigilant not the indolent. Delay sufficient to defeat relief is termed *laches*.

The maxim alerts generally to the dangers of delay and the thinking behind statutes of limitation and the power to strike out for want of prosecution. Lord Denning MR waxed eloquent in condemnation of the law's delays: 'The delay of justice is a denial of justice. Magna Carta will have none of it. "To no one will we deny or delay right or justice." ' All through the years men have protested at the law's delay and counted it as a grievous wrong hard to bear. Shakespeare ranks it among the whips and scorns of time (*Hamlet* Act III. sc. I). Dickens tells how it exhausts finances, patience, courage, hope (*Bleak House*, ch. 1). *Allen* v *Sir Alfred McAlpine* [1968] 2 QB 229 at p. 245.

Vincet veritas 'truth will win'.

Vinculum matrimonii 'the chain *or* bond of marriage'.
See *a vinculo matrimonii*.

Vivat 'may he or she live'. Usually translated as 'long live' as in *vivat Regina,* 'long live the Queen'. These two words appear on a 2006 £5 coin minted for the 80th birthday of HM Queen Elizabeth II (on the reverse above three Royal trumpets). The coin is legal tender (but at a premium!).

Viva voce 'with the living voice', orally. A *viva* is an abbreviation for a *viva voce* examination, i.e. one involving a live and spoken interview. Evidence from the witness box in court is given *viva voce*.

Volenti non fit injuria 'to a willing person no wrong is done'. One who consents to injury cannot be heard to complain and is not in law seen to be injured so as to be entitled to recover damages from one inflicting it. So a boxer or a rugby player will not be entitled to recover in respect of injury inflicted by a fellow sporting participant provided there was nothing malicious or unreasonable in the latter's behaviour. The concept is now however of limited application, being excluded by s. 149 of the Road Traffic Act 1988 in respect of road traffic accidents and for the most part superseded by the law as to contributory negligence (whereby a plaintiff's entitlement to damages for injury caused by another's negligence may be reduced to such extent 'as the court thinks just and equitable according to his share in the responsibility for the damage'. Law Reform (Contributory Negligence) Act 1945 s. 1 (1).)

The case of *Morris* v *Murray* [1990] 3 All ER 801, however, revived the concept. The plaintiff (claimant) and one Murray drank heavily together before getting into a private aircraft piloted by Murray. Due to Murray's drink-related negligence, the plane crashed, killing Murray and seriously injuring Morris. Morris claimed damages against Murray's estate. At first instance the judge gave judgement for Morris and awarded substantial damages less twenty per cent for his contributory negligence in travelling with one whose condition he must have known made him unfit safely to pilot an aeroplane. The Court of Appeal reversed this, holding that, by allowing himself to be so conveyed, he was barred from recovering damages by virtue of *volenti non fit injuria*. Note that, had they travelled together in a motor car, the plaintiff (claimant) would have succeeded (since *volenti non fit injuria* is excluded by the Road Traffic Act) with only a reduction for contributory negligence (possibly as low as twenty per cent on the basis of *Owens* v *Brimmell* [1977] QB 859 but probably substantially higher).

Understandably the layman may think that the 'law is an ass' but abstract justice bearing possibly unconsciously upon the minds of the judges perhaps played its part in the creation of such an apparently absurd inconsistency. This was not a road traffic case and, had Mr Morris succeeded, he would have wiped out the estate of the deceased Murray (who was not apparently insured and was not by law required to be), leaving nothing for his widow. Such a situation cannot arise from road traffic accidents, since the Motor Insurers Bureau agreements provide for claims against uninsured drivers who have committed an offence by being uninsured. Further in *Pitts* v *Hunt* [1991] 1 QB 24 a plaintiff (claimant) passenger failed against a drunken driver where his own participation in the driving was sufficient to involve the maxim *ex turpi causa* (see above).

See *damnum sine injuria esse potest*.

The expression *volenti non fit injuria* used to be seen in defence pleading, e.g., 'The defendant will rely upon *volenti non fit injuria*.' With a ban on the use of Latin some longer version in English will now be necessary e.g.: 'The claimant consented to all acts of the defendant alleged in consequence of which this claim is not maintainable in law.' Note that Bullen and Leake and Jacob's *Precedents of Pleadings* (Sweet and Maxwell, 15th edition, 2004) retains the Latin heading but does not use it in the specimen pleading set out; see vol. 2, 71-S32, p. 1184.

W

With notice see *inter partes*.

Without notice see *ex parte*.

Index